BK 760.903 A234
GRAPHIC ART OF THE EIGHTEENTH CENTURY
/ADHEMAR, J
1964 .00 FV
3000 039313
St. Louis Community College
P9-AOW-549

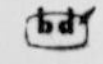

F. Boucher pinxit. J. Janinet sculpsit 1783.

LA TOILETTE DE VENUS

Dédiée à Madame la Comtesse de Coaslin
Née Mailly

GRAPHIC ART OF THE 18TH CENTURY

BY

JEAN ADHÉMAR

McGRAW-HILL BOOK COMPANY
NEW YORK — TORONTO — LONDON

Translated from the French by M. I. Martin

LIBRARY OF CONGRESS CATALOG CARD NUMBER 64-14334

00375

PRINTED IN THE NETHERLANDS

CONTENTS

PREFACE
Page 7

FRANCE IN THE FIRST QUARTER OF THE EIGHTEENTH CENTURY
Page 11

THE ILLUSTRATED BOOK:
OUDRY, BOUCHER, COCHIN, AND THE VIGNETTE ENGRAVERS
Page 29

WILLIAM HOGARTH
Page 60

PAINTER-ETCHERS IN ITALY:
CANALETTO, TIEPOLO AND PIRANESI
Page 71

THE ART OF THE FRENCH PAINTER-ENGRAVERS:
FRAGONARD, SAINT-AUBIN AND THE AMATEURS
Page 91

FRANCE IN THE 'SIXTIES
PROFESSIONAL ENGRAVERS, FIRST ATTEMPTS AT COLOUR, POPULAR PRINTS
Page 120

GERMANY AND ENGLAND
CHODOWIECKI: THE ENGRAVERS AFTER REYNOLDS
Page 143

THE YEARS 1770-89
THE PARIS SCHOOL OF ENGRAVERS:
LAVREINCE, MOREAU-LE-JEUNE, DEBUCOURT
Page 152

THE FRENCH REVOLUTION, GILLRAY, ROWLANDSON
Page 177

GOYA'S CAPRICHOS
Page 201

THE END OF THE CENTURY
Page 214

VARIOUS OPINIONS OF THE PRINTS
OF THE EIGHTEENTH CENTURY,
FROM THEIR OWN DAY UNTIL NOW
Page 230

BIBLIOGRAPHY
Page 237

LIST OF ILLUSTRATIONS
Page 241

INDEX OF NAMES
Page 248

Preface

By the end of the seventeenth century, the art of engraving had been completely mastered. Engravers had at their command two means of expression: line engraving and etching; wood engraving, which had played so distinguished a part in the fifteenth and sixteenth centuries, had almost disappeared. The line engravers reproduced or interpreted the work of other artists; they did not necessarily restrict themselves to the burin alone, but, when it suited their purpose, combined engraving with etching. Some of them were men of considerable artistic talent – a few were painters. The etchers of the seventeenth century, on the other hand – among whom was one great genius, Rembrandt – has an entirely different conception of the print.

The engravers of the eighteenth century were to benefit from this double inheritance. They were helped by particularly favourable social circumstances; the printed image was in use throughout Europe, and it has become the indispensable method of explaining an idea, influencing opinion in political, religious, or social questions, or promoting the sale of every kind of publication. Writers complained of this competition with ill-concealed envy and Mercier, in his *Tableau de Paris,* tells us that there was not a single book, pamphlet or story published without a print: 'The use of engravings in our day is ridiculously overdone.'

Given the political and social conditions in which it was practised, how did engraving develop during the eighteenth century? The virtuosi of the burin continued to interpret the works of others, and reached their highest point of perfection in the course of the century; but in the years following 1789 this kind of print disappeared, along with its public. Paris was to see the production of sensational works; engravers there had by now broken away from their Flemish ancestry and had acquired a specifically French character; in this art, as in literature, France was to influence the whole of Europe. Regional accents persisted, however; for example, one can easily distinguish a print by the German engraver Wille from one by De Launay, though they worked side by side, for the same public, and with the same technique; and the Swede Lavreince, who tried to imitate the Frenchman Baudouin (Boucher's son-in-law), never quite succeeded. Neither Hogarth nor Chodowiecki, though surrounded by French engravers and French prints in London and Dresden respectively, ever lost their national characteristics.

In addition to the great line engravers of the School of Paris, the eighteenth century also witnessed the awakening of nationalist schools in other countries. In England, the mezzotint achieved enormous popularity; it was the medium best suited to the reproduction of Reynolds' great portraits of society beauties. By about 1800 it was in evidence all over Europe, and the schools of Prud'hon and Isabey made excellent use of it. The Italians Tiepolo, Canaletto, and Piranesi were artists of the first rank; the vitality and refinement of their etchings truly left their mark on the century, since Fragonard became their disciple. A revival of etching also took place outside Italy. In France, the 'painter-engravers', both professional and amateur, made their appearance. It may well be that, apart from the Italians and their followers, none of these artists was of more than minor importance, but they prepared the way for the great masters of the nineteenth century. In Spain, Goya made masterly use of the aquatint. This process, invented in England and France, had never been used with any force—except possibly by Gamelin at Toulouse—until the great Spanish genius adopted it at the end of the century. England contributed the art of caricature, also creating, after Hogarth's fumbling experiments, its own mode of expression—the coloured etching. The birth, or re-birth, of caricature—also employed in Switzerland by Huber and in France by Debucourt—was to be of great importance in the political upheavals at the end of the century. Engraving made its appearance in America also; at first, of course, English influence was strong, but this newly-established country quickly developed its own national schools of reproductive and original engraving.

Coming between the very successful seventeenth and nineteenth centuries, the eighteenth century was above all an experimental period, and one of undeniable charm.

This short analysis will help to explain the plan of this book, and the difference between the various chapters. Sometimes the work of a great master has to be analysed, in order to understand his art and to appreciate the particular contribution he has made; on other occasions one must examine a whole movement—a group of artists all working in the same direction, perhaps after analogous models—and here one has to discuss the purport of the movement in general, without dwelling on the various individual artists who contribute to it. Sometimes it may be necessary to devote several pages to a particular series of prints, an illustrated book, or a subject of research, whereas for other matters a line or two may suffice.

We have not given biographies of the engravers. Generally, they led uneventful lives entirely devoted to their work (in those days, a print took anything from a month to three years to execute). The artist's complete absorption in his lengthy task sometimes led to domestic crises—perhaps his wife, not understanding his neglect of her, would feel he was deceiving her with a mistress, whereas he had abandoned her only for his work. There are not many colourful episodes to relate; fortunately for the profession, engravers are not often hanged, like Ryland, for forging bank-notes, or engraving too many of them, or temporarily disgraced, like Balechou, for printing five hundred unauthorised copies his of portrait of the King of Poland, after Rigaud (he was expelled from the Academy, and had to leave France). It is rarely that one finds an eccentric like Etienne Ficquet; he had to engrave a portrait of Mme de Maintenon at the convent of Saint-Cyr, and asked for one of the nuns to keep him company while he worked; the favour was granted, he worked for a month, and then, with a couple of strokes of the burin, destroyed what he had done in order to prolong the pleasant companionship. On the other hand, more than one engraver lost his sight as a result of his work, and others became insane—Gillray, for example, or Drevet *neveu*.

Finally, while giving due credit for fine craftsmanship, little space has been allotted to the reproductive engravers, although they were so highly esteemed in their own day. The author does not agree with an earlier writer who claimed that it was the interpreters who gave the French eighteenth-century print its richness and brilliance. Close attention will be paid here to the work of the original engravers, and the designers of illustrations; Moreau *le jeune* and Cochin *fils* will occupy a more important place than the engravers who reproduced their work.

Before embarking on this book, I wish to acknowledge with gratitude my indebtedness to many friends and colleagues: in France, MM. Roux, Pognon, Dacier, Weigert, Bruand, and Mlle Hébert; in Italy, Mr Hind and Signor Palluchini; in the United States, Mr Hyatt Major, Mr Zigrosser, Mr Lopez-Rey, and Mr Huxley; in Spain, Señora Paez de Santiago, Señor Lafuente Ferrari; in England, Mr Watson, Mr Basil Gray, Mrs George. I should also like to thank M. Paul Prouté, who has very kindly made a number of helpful suggestions.

FRANCE IN THE FIRST QUARTER OF THE EIGHTEENTH CENTURY

From the point of view of the arts, the eighteenth century really begins, not with the year 1700, but somewhere about 1710. This was the time of Louis XIV's old age, yet, a time also of rejuvenation; it was, on the one hand, the period of Watteau's etchings, so new and so perfect, for all their unstudied air, and on the other, the period of Law's Mississippi scheme which, by causing the ruin of one section of society was to bring into power a new class, a new and less cultivated but shrewder public, determined to enjoy its new prosperity with the least possible delay and, in consequence, demanding new forms of expression in the arts.

In this chapter, I shall confine my remarks to France, since that country, and Paris in particular, gave the lead during these years, and in every field Watteau was the dominant figure.

At the beginning of the eighteenth century, some of the French painters of *fêtes galantes* began to develop an interest in *la gravure de peintre*—engraving executed by the painter himself as an extension of his skill as a draughtsman into a different field and for a different purpose. This movement lasted only a short time, and was hardly known to the general public; but its effects were far reaching, and thirty years later a similar development took place, again in France, and this time with greater success. During the period 1700-1710, however, 'engravings' were generally accepted to mean reproductions of whatever paintings happened to be fashionable, whether by old masters or by contemporary artists; these were made either to introduce such paintings to a wider public or to help sell them.

Of course, there had been painter-engravers ever since the fifteenth century in the Low Countries and in Italy—even in France, among some of the major artists who came back from Italy; but their numbers were limited, although their works are in the first rank and they include men such as Dürer, Rembrandt, Claude, Callot, and the anonymous French artist of *L'Abusé en cour* (late fifteenth century). The revival of original engraving early in the eighteenth century must have been brought about, one feels, by the encouragement of someone who knew and collected the work of Callot, La Fage, and Rembrandt; such an individual existed in Paris in the person of Pierre Mariette, print dealer and

ANTOINE WATTEAU. *Italian Costumes.* 1st state

ANTOINE WATTEAU. *Departure of the Italian Actors.*
Engraved by L. Jacob

publisher, whose shop in the Rue Saint-Jacques was well stocked and much frequented. Mme Adhémar and M. Weigert have been able to prove that this collection was formed for pleasure rather than for commerce, because he had gathered it together before such works had become fashionable. It may well be that he persuaded more than one painter to take up the etching needle—in particular, Watteau; his son, Pierre-Jean, did the same for Octavien. Outside Mariette's circle, artists' etchings were little sought after and although these delightful prints

ANTOINE WATTEAU. *Costume Study*

were 'finished' works in their own right, they were regarded as mere preparations or rough ideas, to be completed by professional engravers with the burin.

In about 1710, Watteau etched a series of costume subjects; the series contains only ten plates instead of the usual twelve, which suggests that for some reason its production was interrupted. It was less successful than the dull fashion plates by Bonnart, which appeared regularly every year—even every season. Watteau also drew two of his own paintings on copper: *Marching Troops* and *The Italian Comedy.* The

ANTOINE WATTEAU. *Seated Woman*

latter, of which only one etched proof is known, was 'finished' by Simonneau. It may have been Claude Gillot, Watteau's first teacher, who persuaded him to take up etching. Gillot was also a friend of Mariette, and produced etchings of fantastic subjects—satyrs, orgies and so on—in the tradition of Callot.

Quillard (1701-1733), Octavien, Pater, Philippe Mercier—in fact, all the painters of *fêtes galantes* except Lancret—also made etchings with the character of jottings of freely-drawn sketches, particularly of fashion subjects.

ANTOINE WATTEAU. *A Ride on a Sledge.* Engraved by Boucher

As well as making an important contribution to the history of etching, Watteau also helped (this time involuntarily) in the development of reproductive engraving and in the course of the eighteenth century 750 reproductive prints were made after his paintings. As early as 1719, his most famous paintings had already been engraved by several craftsmen, who no doubt shared their profits with the artist, as was the usual custom.

Then, in 1726, there appeared an engraved collection of his drawings, and, from 1721 to 1734, a collection of engravings after his best paintings. The latter, therefore, was published after his death; the plates were begun in 1721, when his success was at its height, and were completed with some difficulty in 1734, at a time when other artists, particularly de Troy, had ousted him from public favour.

This series of engravings was due to the initiative of one man alone – Jean de Jullienne. Jullienne was a friend of Watteau during the artist's final years; they probably met through Crozat, the art patron, or at the shop of one of the Paris print-dealers in the rue Saint-Jacques. Jullienne himself was a great lover of painting, and the Director of the Gobelins; he became fanatically devoted to Watteau, bought a great many of his paintings, subsequently selling them to wealthy collectors among his acquaintances. In order to make a record of these paintings before their inevitable dispersal, he employed the only means at his disposal; whereas we would now have them photographed by experts, he had them engraved, and the collection of prints thus produced is known as

ANTOINE WATTEAU. *Recruits going to join the Regiment*

ANTOINE WATTEAU. *The Anxious Sweetheart*

the *Recueil Jullienne.* It consists of about two hundred engravings, in two volumes—the first contains the upright pictures and the second those of landscape format. The work was not published by subscription as Jullienne was against this, and met all the expenses of publication himself. He sold proofs of the plates separately, as they came out (mostly in 1728 and 1729); he made no profit out of the undertaking, because although the first plates sold well, the later ones did not. Jullienne completed the series of paintings by a collection of 351 engravings after the drawings: the *Figures de différents caractères.*

There are several points worth noting in connection with the *Recueil Jullienne.* To begin with, it was a private undertaking, unique of its kind, the enterprise of a man with enough intelligence and perception to recognize a great artist, and to aim at reproducing his entire *œuvre,* without any particular thought of personal gain. Artists such as Rubens had already had their own works reproduced in engravings, and others (Rigaud, for example) were to do so later, but no other art lover was ever to emulate Jullienne. His friend Crozat (who also knew Watteau) did indeed consider having engravings made of all the drawings in his collection (the finest in France), but the plan was too ambitious, and came to nothing. However, the *Recueil Jullienne* initiated a whole series of engravings illustrating the pictures in various museums, galleries and private collections *(Cabinet Poullain, Galerie du Palais-Royal, Galerie du Luxembourg, Galerie du comte de Brühl,* etc.). It set a fashion for such things, and pointed the way to the King of France, though the masterpieces in the Louvre were not engraved till much later, and then only very badly. The *Galerie de Florence* was published at the end of the century, engraved by Lacombe and Masquelier after drawings by Wicar (first instalment in 1789, fiftieth in 1821).

Almost all the important engravers of the period were employed in the production of the *Recueil Jullienne,* partly, no doubt, to encourage a spirit of competition among them, but also in order to be able to complete it more quickly. The work would never have been finished if it had been left to a single engraver. Nearly all of them were professionals such as Ch. Simonneau, Gaspard Duchange, Jean Audran and Tardieu, but the team also included the young Boucher, who engraved more than twenty plates. They worked at the Gobelins, Jullienne's premises, where he fed and housed them, supervised them, and no

NICOLAS LANCRET. *Quoi n'avez-vous point?...*
Engraved by M. Horthemels, wife of Cochin *père*

NICOLAS LANCRET. *Dans cette Aimable Solitude…*
Engraved by Cochin *père*

CHARLES-NICOLAS COCHIN PÈRE. *Le Jeu du Pied de Bœuf.*
Engraved after de Troy

doubt gave them the benefit of his advice, backed by his authority as a wealthy man and his discernment as an amateur etcher. Jullienne's personal taste is of great interest, because it influenced engraving techniques; in fact, a new technique had to be found, since Watteau's pictures could not be engraved in the same style as those of Lebrun. Painted with greater freedom, they demanded a similar freedom in the engraving. Pure line engraving was too austere, and Jullienne rejected mezzotint, though this was fashionable at the time and might have produced a satisfactory rendering of the paintings. Probably at the suggestion of Audran, whose family had used the method, it was decided to make a preparatory etching, rapidly sketched in on the copper, and work over with the burin, accenting it where necessary. This was a technical innovation of much interest, because it was subsequently used throughout the entire eighteenth century.

So the *Recueil Jullienne* was put together, and also the *Figures de différents caractères.* They enjoyed considerable success, adorning the walls of French homes throughout the eighteenth century, and remaining popular for several generations. They were copied and imitated on a smaller scale by Chéreau and Bernard Picart, who used vast numbers of them as designs for box-lids, screens and fans. Hundreds of painted copies were also made, and certified to be 'true copies of the prints'. They were immensely successful in Germany, and played an important part in the diffusion of baroque art; Martin Engelbrecht of Augsburg specialised in producing ponderous coloured replicas of plates from the *Recueil Jullienne.* These plates became fashionable in England, but they had no success in Italy.

Similar engravings were made after works by Watteau's followers; we shall confine ourselves to those after de Troy and Lemoyne. De Troy was very much liked by 'respectable but tender-hearted' ladies of the Paris bourgeoisie (see his biography by the Chevalier de Valory). Between 1708 and 1731 he painted what were then known as *sujets de modes* – attractive and elegant scenes of comtemporary life intended for a new type of clientele: financiers who had grown rich through speculation at the end of Louis XIV's reign. De Troy did a great deal of work for patrons of this kind, such as the well-known Samuel Bernard and Lalive, Receveur Général des Finances (he painted thirty-two overdoors for the latter around 1726). A great many large engravings were made after

JEAN-MARC NATTIER. *Night departs and Dawn appears.*
Engraved by Pierre Maleuvre

his paintings, in addition to the painted replicas. They enjoyed a considerable reputation, thanks to the skill of their authors, of whom Cochin *père* (1688-1754) was the most famous. In 1735 the latter engraved *Le Jeu du Pied de Bœuf* (line engraving over a preparatory etching), and insisted on putting the date of the painting (1725) at the foot, and not that of the engraving, 'on account of the costumes and manners' which it was intended to illustrate. This well-known and very fine engraving depicts a frivolous and, so they say, corrupt society, rediscovering a taste for childish pleasures in a delightful garden near Paris.

Lemoyne's paintings were usually engraved by Laurent Cars, a member of one of the numerous dynasties of engravers flourishing in the eighteenth century, which guaranteed the continuance of a tradition in creating a somewhat academic style. They mostly originated at about the beginning of the seventeenth century and lasted till the revolution, after which they disappeared. The Cars family was one of the most distinguished of these dynasties, and can be studied as a typical example of how they attained success, flourished for a period, and then declined.

The ancestor of this family of artists was a certain Jean Cars, a painter, working in Paris in about 1630. He married Marthe Firens, daughter of the publisher Pierre Firens, who had originally come from Antwerp, and worked in Paris in the rue Saint-Jacques, at the sign of *L'Imprimerie en taille-douce.* He claimed to have introduced copper engraving to France, replacing the traditional wood block. According to M.R.A. Weigert's researches, Firens had a son (or a nephew) named Gaspard who was an engraver, one of his daughters married the painter Paufi, and the other married the engraver Charles David. Jean Cars was the father of François, an engraver of books, who settled in Lyon; probably also of Gabriel Cars, who worked in Lyon in the seventeenth century. François had fifteen children, one of them, Jean-François, was born in Lyon in 1670 and died in Paris in 1730. Jean-François, working in the tradition of Nanteuil and Edelinck, engraved portraits and, more particularly, illustrated theses. These two activities go together because, in the seventeenth and eighteenth centuries a thesis was not a book; rather it resembled a large printed handbill, setting out the propositions and ideas which the candidate intented to defend when he presented his thesis, and was surmounted by a portrait of the distinguished patron, to whom the thesis was dedicated. Nanteuil made engravings for a great number of such theses, and Cars succeeded him as a specialist in this type of portrait.

Jean-François Cars had a son, Laurent; this is the person with whom we are now concerned. He was born in Lyon, where his family still lived in 1699; then his father moved to Paris, and took the boy with him. He was apprenticed to Christophe, a minor painter of the period. His parents wanted him to be a painter, because it was a more highly esteemed profession than engraving, and possibly also a more lucrative one. His heredity was against him, however—there were at least three engravers in his grandparents' generation, and several more among his uncles; it was therefore more or less inevitable that he should become an engraver as well. He began work in this medium about 1723, and continued till 1750. According to Grimm, he then abandoned engraving and became a print dealer. In particular, he continued to benefit from the very large stock of theses left to him by his father, disposing of the best of them to the Jesuit colleges.

Cars worked for a comparatively short period, therefore—only twenty-five years, which is not very long. It is not known who taught him, he most likely began his training under his father, and was probably also sent to study with Audran, like his older compatriot Drevet. Gérard Audran, the skilful interpreter of Le Brun's paintings, was a very celebrated engraver whose name was mentioned only with the very greatest respect in eighteenth-century studios. The engraver Le Bas, whom we shall meet again later, always referred to him with veneration, and when he spoke of 'l'immortel M. Audran' he used to raise his hat as a sign of esteem. Audran's style is rather more free than that of Nanteuil, though still very classical in character. Laurent Cars inherited Audran's manner; it is with Audran that he was compared, and the writers of the day rated him very highly, placing him on a level with Drevet. Cochin says that his plates are 'supérieurement gravées'; and Watelet describes him as the best engraver of his day.

Laurent Cars was not primarily a portrait engraver, and made lively and elegant prints after Watteau's *fêtes galantes,* such as the *Fêtes Vénitiennes.* He is known above all as the engraver of Lemoyne's paintings, of which he produced about a dozen prints. We do not know enough about his life to say whether the two men were friends, and

The villager. Engraved by Guérard

whether Lemoyne helped and advised Cars as Rigaud had helped Drevet. It is not very likely; Cars seems to have worked alone, possibly enjoying higher standing than Drevet. Lempereur, an amateur who has left an account of the engraving of that period, remarks that Cars seems more likely to have been the creator of this work than a mere copyist. His aim was not simply to be a craftsman, a kind of photographer, but to give his personal interpretation of the subject.

His most important engravings are of three pictures by Lemoyne, and date from 1728; but Lemoyne died in 1737, and in any case Cars did not work exclusively after this artist. In 1731 he engraved *La Camargo dansant,* after Lancret—a print which was sold all over Europe—and the King of France commissioned him to make an engraving of *Mlle Clairon en Médée,* after Van Loo, which he wished to offer to the actress. Cars carries out the engraving very successfully except for the head, which he had to entrust to Beauvarlet; he could not undertake it himself because the plate was a very large one and he was extremely short-sighted. He also executed plates after paintings by Chardin and Greuze. In 1771 he died, but the best of his work survives in the three plates of 1728 after Lemoyne: *Hercules and Omphale, Perseus and Andromeda* and *The Annuciation.*

Another professional portrait engraver of the period is Pierre-Imbert Drevet. His father, Pierre Drevet, studied under the Audrans, did engravings after Rigaud's paintings, and left Lyon to settle in Paris. Pierre-Imbert was born in 1697 and died in 1739 at the age of forty-one. Edmond Pognon regards his *Bossuet,* after Rigaud (1723), as a work of genius; it is one of the most celebrated plates in the history of the print, and fifteen different states of it exist. Unfortunately, Drevet was attacked by mental illness when he was about thirty, and was never able to develop his talent more fully. The *Bossuet* of 1723 is therefore not only a masterpiece but also a swan song; the culmination of a genre which was already doomed to extinction. It was soon to be supplanted by the fashion for portraits on a small scale, and photography ultimately made it disappear altogether. A few more examples of this type of portrait were executed in about 1760; but it is now time to turn to the engraved illustration of the eighteenth century, which also originated in Paris, and whose beginnings can be said to date from the same year as Drevet's *Bossuet* (1723).

THE ILLUSTRATED BOOK - OUDRY, BOUCHER, COCHIN, AND THE VIGNETTE ENGRAVERS

The eighteenth century was one of the most remarkable periods in the history of illustration. Never have artists interpreted literary texts with more skill and elegance, or succeeded in conveying the spirit of them with greater intelligence and taste. This feeling for small-scale work, so characteristic a part of the eighteenth century, was eminently suited to books, which at that time were becoming pocket-sized volumes for light reading. Ladies had their portraits painted with such a book either in their hand, or laid on a nearby table, and gentlemen, when out walking, carried one in their muff or their pocket.

Typographically, of course, there was still some way to go, for text and illustration were not yet combined on one page, as was done later, in the nineteenth century. Small engravings were simply inserted here and there in the book, because the copper plates could not be printed at the same time as the type pages. This was the only weakness of the illustrated books of the period; we shall now consider some of the best examples.

The transition from the seventeenth to the eighteenth century was brought about by Bernard Picart (1673-1733), a delightful minor master who illustrated a number of books. He was a protestant, which is one reason why he was obliged to leave France at the end of the seventeenth century. Another reason was the increasing difficulty of making a living in Paris towards 1710; commissions were hard to obtain. He left France, therefore, and settled in Holland, in Amsterdam, where he sold prints and made drawings for illustrations. At that time Holland was a paradise for the bookseller and the illustrator. The religious and political freedom it enjoyed made possible the publication of all kinds of subversive or slightly scandalous books which sold well everywhere in Europe—a state of affairs which lasted throughout the eighteenth century. Bernard Picart published and illustrated a book of this kind: *Cérémonies et Coutumes religieuses de tous les peuples du monde représentées par des figures, avec des explications,* etc. (1723-1743).

This work, which seems to foreshadow the French *philosophes,* was intended to demonstrate in a subtle, indirect way that Christianity was not the only religion in the world, and with that object in view it

JEAN-BAPTISTE OUDRY. *Deer at Bay*

JEAN-BAPTISTE OUDRY. *The Frogs who wanted a King.*
.llustration for La Fontaine's *Fables*. Engraved by Chedel.

FRANÇOIS BOUCHER. *Pensent-ils au raisin?* Engraved by J. P. Le Bas

compared Christian ceremonies with those of other religions and with the most extraordinary superstitions. The book was enormously successful; it played an important part in eighteenth-century anti-clerical propaganda; pirated editions came out in Paris in 1741 and 1783; Picart's plates were published again in Paris in 1810 and 1819.

Picart was the ideal artist for this type of pictorial illustration, because he had drawn a great many costume plates when he was in Paris. He also illustrated Boileau's *Le Lutrin, Les Aventures de Télémaque,* and above all *Les Métamorphoses d'Ovide* (1732).

Claude Gillot is another minor master who worked at the end of the seventeenth and the beginning of the eighteenth centuries. He had the

Les Précieuses ridicules. Illustration for Molière by Boucher.
Engraved by L. Cars

FRANÇOIS BOUCHER. *The Charms of Country Life.*
Engraved by J. Daullé

FRANÇOIS BOUCHER. *Girl resting.* 1736

CHARLES-NICOLAS COCHIN FILS. *The Ladies' Tailor.* 1737

CHARLES-NICOLAS COCHIN FILS. *Madame du Deffand's Persian Cats*

distinction of being Watteau's master, and transmitted some of his qualities to the latter. He illustrated La Motte's *Fables,* published in Paris in 1719. Dedicated to Louis XV, they had little literary merit, owing their fame to Gillot's illustrations. These are pleasing compositions, reminiscent of the same artist's paintings with their elongated, elegant, dancing figures. Unfortunately, his drawing of animals is weak. Two editions of the work appeared in 1719: a quarto edition with illustrations by Gillot, Coypel and others, and a duodecimo edition with the pictures drawn and engraved by Gillot himself.

In about 1730, the great animal artist Oudry, who did much work for the Court and for the royal manufactories, executed numerous drawings connected with La Fontaine's *Fables.* He had thought of using them for tapestries when the opportunity presented itself, but when he died in 1755 they were bought by a collector, M. de Montenault, who planned to use them to illustrate an edition of the *Fables.* The drawings (now in

CHARLES-NICOLAS COCHIN FILS. *Funeral of the Dauphine, Maria Teresa of Spain.* 1748

America) are mere sketches and jottings, pleasant but unfinished. Montenault could not, therefore, have them engraved just as they were. So he sought the advice of several bibliophiles, and of the vignette artist Cochin. The latter has left us an account of this bibliophiles' conference over the design of the book. They gravely discussed questions of no importance, and failed to reach an agreement; one of

CHARLES-NICOLAS COCHIN FILS. *An Experiment with Electricity.* *c.* 1739

them was so scatter-brained that the others had to keep repeating to him everything that had just been said; another was terribly self-important; a third, 'a complete simpleton, agreed with everyone in turn'. Finally, the whole matter was handed over to Cochin. He put the drawings into shape, and produced more finished versions of them; he then etched them, and finally had the plates completed with the burin. The little scenes are excellent, the landscapes full of charm and the interiors renowned for their quality. There is great ingenuity in the compositions,

CHARLES-NICOLAS COCHIN FILS. *The Patcher. c.* 1737.
Engraved by Ravenet

but, oddly enough, some of the animals are not altogether successful. It should be observed that wood engraving, at that time largely abandoned, plays an important part in the book; the fleurons are by the wood engraver Papillon, to whom we shall return later.

Another beautiful book was the *Œuvres* of Molière, illustrated by Boucher. We shall be studying the drawings of this painter of *scènes galantes* in greater detail, since they were engraved in colour by Demarteau. Boucher did about thirty illustrations for the six in-folio volumes of Molière's plays, published in 1734. An illustrated edition of Molière had already been produced in 1682 but Boucher's edition is perhaps the best of all, and the only one that arouses any enthusiasm. At the beginning of each play, he depicts a characteristic scene, and the whole

CHARLES-NICOLAS COCHIN FILS. *Mésangère Sale Catalogue*

CHARLES-NICOLAS COCHIN FILS. *The Genie of Medals. c.* 1737

is perfect in feeling and perception. The engravings are by Laurent Cars, whom we have already met as an interpreter of Lemoyne. These illustrations are charming, carefree compositions, treated in an eighteenth-century style, and in the costume of that period, with none of the passion for archaeological exactitude common at the end of the century. Boucher depicts the comedies as he had seen them acted, and his figures are reminiscent of those of Watteau (he had done some engravings after Watteau a little earlier). The book was large and costly. A smaller edition, with Boucher's drawings reduced in size, appeared in Amsterdam in 1741. We see in this the beginning of a trend towards small-scale engraving and the work of the vignettists, which was to replace engraving after the work of painters.

Charles-Nicolas Cochin (1715-1790), known as Cochin *fils,* whom we have just met as adviser to bibliophiles, is the most prolific vignette artist in France of the eighteenth century, and also one of the best. His name is synonymous with the vignettes of this period, in fact, these small illustrations were invariably called *des Cochin* in the time of Louis XV.

Cochin belonged to a family of engravers. His father executed plates after Watteau and the other masters of the time, and some of his forebears were engraving devotional pictures at Troyes in the sixteenth century. Therefore with a continuous tradition behind him, he, too, was destined to become an engraver, but the type of work done by his father seemed very dull to him. Instead of reproductive engravings, which were very slow to do, he preferred more freely executed, rapid sketches, engraved by himself after his own original drawings. We have already seen that he reproduced Oudry's compositions for La Fontaine's *Fables,* but to him this was simply a job of work; what he really enjoyed doing was his own drawings and vignettes. He excelled at these, and his career was a brilliant one. He started engraving when he was twelve, and became an associate of the Academy when he was barely twenty-six, having already, at the age of twenty-four, been appointed draughtsman and engraver to the Cabinet du Roi. In 1749, aged thirty-four, he accompanied the Directeur des Beaux-Arts to Italy. The latter went to admire the works of the Italian masters, at that time considered an indispensable experience. He took with him the architect Soufflot, an art critic, the Abbé Leblanc, and Cochin, to prompt him as to what he ought to think about them. Cochin's career was greatly helped by this journey, on which he proved to be a most entertaining companion. The Directeur des Beaux-Arts happened to be the brother of Madame de Pompadour, and in high favour with Louis XV at the time, so when he returned to France, in 1751, Cochin was made an *Académicien* at the age of thirty-six, and at thirty-seven he was keeper of the Cabinet du Roi. He continued as adviser to Marigny, the Directeur des Beaux-Arts, and became his assistant in charge of what he called the *canal des grâces,* or distribution of patronage.

Tiré du Cabinet de Monsieur Baudouin Peintre du Roy

Although he died in 1790, at an advanced age, he had ceased to produce any work after about 1751, but spent his time drawing, writing about art, and enjoying the pleasures of life (he never married, which was most unusual at that period).

Here is how his contemporary, Bachaumont, sums him up: 'M. Cochin *fils* is what one might describe as a very *pretty* engraver. His drawing is attractive, pleasing, graceful, of great delicacy and lightness. His art is facile and elegant. He is a very prolific artist and shows great skill in design and composition, but his work is almost entirely on a very small scale. He has done a great deal of engraving: nearly all the fêtes at Versailles and Paris, a large number of vignettes, frontispieces and plates for books.' This is a very just appreciation of Cochin's talent, and several points from it are worth remembering: the *prettiness* of his work; the fact that he only worked *en petit* (the days of heroic engraving, the plates of Audran, and the grand manner, were gone); and finally, his engraving of fêtes and the frontispieces of hundreds of little books.

As an engraver of festivals he is without equal, and it is perhaps here that he is seen at his best. From 1739 he was associated with the Soldtz brothers, the decorators in charge of the *Menus Plaisirs.* He helped them in the vast schemes they carried out for all the court festivities, and for weddings and funerals, and engraved the decorations for the handsome albums which commemorated these events. This was the kind of work he liked; he had already shown a taste for it in 1729, at the age of fourteen, in an engraving of a firework display in the Piazza Navona in Rome, after Pannini. In 1741 he engraved the decorative scheme constructed by the Soldtz brothers in Notre Dame for the funeral of the Dauphine. M. de Bonneval, superintendant of the *Menus Plaisirs,* demanded that his own name should appear at the bottom as the designer of the engraving. 'Everyone laughed at this', says Cochin, 'and no-one was taken in by it, but he was quite satisfied.' This brings us into contact with a characteristic aspect of the eighteenth century. Fashionable society was not content simply with patronising the arts, with buying paintings and acquiring an appreciation for them, it wished to produce works of art itself.

LOUIS-MARIN BONNET. *Head of a Woman.* Engraved after Boucher

HUBERT-FRANÇOIS GRAVELOT. *Electricity*

In 1745, Cochin designed three plates showing the festivities in honour of the Dauphin's wedding at Versailles. His mother had helped with the engraving of the 1729 plate, but with these his father assisted him, for Cochin realized that it would be a waste of his own time to carry out the routine burin work, and he simply drew the design on the plate with the drypoint or the etching needle. These engravings for the Dauphin's wedding are his most successful works, closely followed by the *Masked Ball in the Galerie des Glaces* and the *Fancy Dress Ball in the Petite Ecurie.*

In 1746 he produced plates illustrating the funeral of the Dauphine at Notre Dame, and her burial at Saint-Denis. These are signed by the Soldtz brothers, who were very good at designing festivals, but really surpassed themselves at funerals. 'They have been criticised for giving everything a flavour of gallantry, and a somewhat unsuitably festive air... but they aimed to please the Court, which was against too much seriousness in any circumstances – and they were not unsuccessful.'

After this, ceremonies became rare events, and the state of the Treasury was such that it could no longer afford to have engravings made of them, so Cochin turned to book illustration. He had already been interested in it for some time; in 1741, at the age of twenty-six, he had formed a friendship with the great publisher Jombert, who had immediately appreciated his worth, given him commissions, and launched him on this career. Jombert made a collection of almost the whole of Cochin's *œuvre,* and produced a catalogue of it.

Cochin preferred to do the frontispiece of a book, rather than vignettes. He worked unremittingly, because he needed the money, and also because he found a delight in satisfying his strong creative urge and fertile imagination. Some of his output he etched himself, the rest he drew in pencil or sanguine, and left the engraving to a colleague.

HUBERT-FRANÇOIS GRAVELOT. *The Absent-minded Man.*
Illustration for an edition of La Bruyère

CHARLES-DOMINIQUE EISEN. *Vignette.* Engraved by J. de Longueil

His frontispieces are innumerable, and were highly esteemed in his own day. Diderot called him 'the leading French draughtsman'. He did not usually illustrate novels, but serious works—classics, devotional books, treatises on war and the military arts, and so on. As the Goncourts have so well shown, he gave all these a pretty, stylish air which their subjects in truth lacked: 'Cochin is the artist who has lent charm to science. He has the wit, the ingenuity, the lightness of touch of another Fontanelle. He is without an equal... for showing crowds of cherubs

CHARLES-DOMINIQUE EISEN. *Vignette.* Engraved by J. de Longueil

sliding down a pair of compasses, amid clouds and flowers..., or adorning even the horrors of war with gay little tail-pieces, and transforming the explosion of a shell or a mine into a drawing as pleasing to the eye as a decorative box-lid of the period.'

He had a passion for allegories and emblems – Time, Death, Religion, and so on – and produced endless variations on these themes. He has been severely criticised on this point; Louis Réau accuses him of overdoing these 'childish and nonsensical refuses'. Even in his own

PIERRE-PHILIPPE CHOFFARD. *Allegory*. Engraved by Gautier-Dagoty

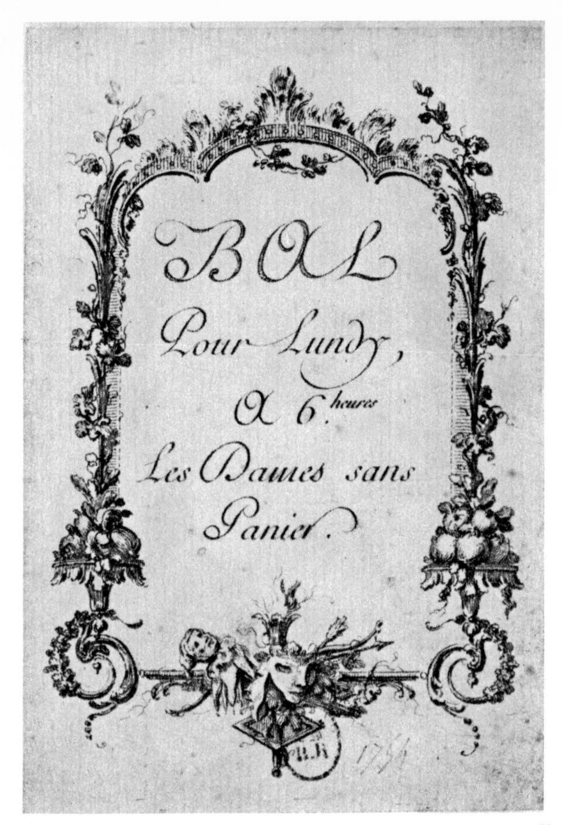

PIERRE-PHILIPPE CHOFFARD. *Vignette for a Ball*

day, Diderot (who admired him, as we have seen) also found fault with him for having 'too many ideas, dragging allegory into everything, and thus spoiling and confusing his work'. In spite of all this, however, Cochin remains one of the finest draughtsmen of his day.

Another vignettist, older than Cochin but working during the same period, was Hubert Gravelot (1699-1773). Gravelot was the son of a tailor; his father wished to give him the education of a gentleman, but all Gravelot wanted to do was to draw. He was also very pleasure-loving, in fact, he was somewhat wild, and was packed off to the island of San Domingo when he was quite young, in an attempt to reform him. He stayed there several years, but the experience did not leave any

JEAN DAULLÉ. *Louis XV, King of France.* Engraved after Rigaud

mark on him. Then he returned to Paris, was unable to make a name there, and in 1732, at the age of thirty-three, he left France and came to England. We know little or nothing about the illustrations he executed in England, which is a pity, because it would be interesting to discover whether he introduced the latest French style here, or was himself influenced by English taste. He stayed in London till 1745, when he was forty-six, then he returned to Paris. This time he was immediately successful – no easy matter during the height of Cochin's triumph. But he was not as productive as Cochin; he was lazy, or (as the Goncourts put it) he had acquired a taste for leisure while he was in England—a taste for time to do what he liked, time for relaxation. There was none of Cochin's frenzied activity about him. He liked obscurity; he was never talked about, and never exhibited his work anywhere. He stayed at home reading, burying himself in his books; he was an avid reader, and took what he read so seriously that he used to weep, even to sob aloud, over his book. It was an over-sentimental age, when tears flowed readily.

Nevertheless he found time to engrave. His most active period was roughly between 1745 and 1762 then he suffered his first bereavement, and his grief, together with failing sight, forced him to give up working. He drew vignettes, one for each book to be illustrated; he also did the illustrations for three large books: the *Decameron* of Boccaccio (London, 1757), Marmontel's *Contes* (Paris, 1765), and *La Nouvelle Héloïse* (Amsterdam, 1761).

His illustrations have great charm, and a special kind of elegance. He is wonderful at representing interiors; he handles only trivial subjects, and with a more marked spirit of *galanterie* than Cochin; but his work is saved by its air of distinction. There is a well known letter in which he asks a collector 'how far one should go with one's jesting, because although refinement is always preferable to coarseness in this kind of composition, some people, as you know, must have partridges, and others must have lumps of butchers' meat'.

Charles Eisen (1720-1778) was Flemish, and perhaps more alive and more direct than a pair of exquisites like Cochin and Gravelot. His temperament is reflected in the vigour and robustness of his work. Gravelot may have been wild, but Eisen was worse—a real libertine, whose debauchery shocked his contemporaries even in that far from prudish century.

He was born at Valenciennes, in Watteau's country. His father was a painter from Brussels, and took charge of the boy's education himself, setting him to work, and taking him to study the masters in various private collections. Eisen stayed at Valenciennes till he was about twenty, then in 1741 he went to Paris (where Cochin's first vignettes were just appearing) and entered the studio of Le Bas, a reproductive engraver who was much esteemed at the time, and whose studio was full of young artists, both French and foreign. His first prints appeared in about 1747, and he went on working till 1770.

We will confine ourselves here to three of his most important works. In 1753 *Premier livre d'une œuvre suivie* appeared, a collection of decorative motifs. It was the work of a designer of ornaments, like that of Lajoue and Meissonier later, but on a small scale, in the form of vignettes. These compositions provided a fund of ideas for contemporary artists. Goncourt expressed great admiration for the series, saying that Eisen had produced, 'as it were, the complete album of *rocaille* studies'.

In 1762 another work was published—a very famous one—the *Contes* of La Fontaine, an edition sponsored by the *fermiers généraux* (tax-farmers). These important and powerful people were responsible for the collection of taxes in France, and were both influential and rich. They had not yet acquired very much polish, there was much of the *nouveau riche* about them. They enjoyed a *risqué* story, a slightly coarse jest—in fact, the 'butchers' meat' mentioned by Gravelot. They got together to commission an illustrated book, thus forming one of the first societies of bibliophiles. They entrusted to one of their number, M. d'Agincourt, the task of selecting the artists, the paper, and the type face. He approached Eisen; Eisen made drawings, several of his colleagues (principally Le Mire and Longueuil) engraved the plates, and the ornaments were by Choffard, a vignettist whom we shall encounter again later. 'The plates designed by M. Eisen', proclaims an announcement, 'express without obscenity the most piquant moments in the *Contes.* In some we perceive the touch of Rubens, in others that of Teniers, and in nearly all the touch of the Graces,' Eisen's Flemish background is thus clearly indicated and clearly seen.

The book was published in a fairly large edition, some of the copies with *figures libres* (extra plates whose subject-matter was of a somewhat 'free' nature). It was reprinted in the same year without the tail-pieces; in 1764 there was an edition with Amsterdam given as the town of origin and copies of the 1762 illustrations.

In 1770 another book was published with illustrations by Eisen—Dorat's *The Kisses*—the last of the three we have selected by this artist. The poetry is third-rate, and no-one reads it, but the vignettes are delightful, and the book was bought for their sake; they were 'free' in

JEAN-MICHEL PAPILLON. *Vignette engraved on Wood*

character, with a touch of vulgarity. Grimm wrote: 'Monsieur Dorat has presented to us for spring a very spring-like book called *The Kisses,* with so many vignettes and fleurons that it could be regarded as a work by Charles Eisen, the illustrator, rather than by Joseph Dorat, who wrote the verses.'

Dorat's *The Kisses* is, as it were, the culmination of book illustration in eighteenth-century France. The illustration 'kills' the text, which is nothing but a pretext for the pictures, an almost useless appendage. Soon, in the early nineteenth century, books devoted to engravings appeared, either with or without a text. In 1825, for example, a work was published which was announced as follows: *Les Amours de Psyché et de Cupidon, lithographies... sous la direction de Monsieur Castel-Courval,*

PIERRE-IMBERT DREVET. *Bossuet.* Engraved after Rigaud

édition ornée du poème de La Fontaine sur le sujet. The bibliographer Brunet, on reading this title, wrote indignantly: 'So far, we have had numbers of poems adorned with engravings, but it has been left to Monsieur Castel de Courval to give us some engravings adorned with a poem.' But it was too late to protest, Brunet was left behind, the evolution continued, and the luxury books produced to-day are the result.

All the artists we have considered so far produced vignettes characteristic of the Louis XV period; although some of them lived till the beginning of the nineteenth century, their most interesting period of activity hardly ever extended beyond 1760 or 1770. We now come to the illustration of Louis XVI's reign. Louis XVI came to the throne in 1774, but the style associated with his name made its appearance a little earlier in about 1770, and lasted till about 1780. There were not so many artists working during those years. The indefatigable Cochin still had a few years to go; Marillier had begun working (his *chef-d'œuvre* was Dorat's *Fables* of 1773); and there were a few others who have recently been brought out, somewhat undeservedly, from the comparative obscurity in which they should have been allowed to remain.

Finally, mention should be made of Choffard (1730-1809). He was a designer of ornaments, and an admirable engraver of tail-pieces, borders and dedications. He began work in 1749, when he was nineteen. In 1762, he did fifty-three tail-pieces for Eisen's edition of La Fontaine's *Contes,* and he never surpassed these, though he went on engraving till 1789. In 1804 he published his very enjoyable *Notice sur l'art de la gravure,* defending the artistic rights of France against England.

Wood engraving, which had been very popular in the sixteenth century, had fallen into decline by this period. Wood blocks were regarded simply as a way of providing fairly cheap decorative prints, and were considered inferior to the copper processes. Wood engravers did not try to recapture the effects achieved by their sixteenth-century precursors, and for technical reasons they were still unable to produce the brilliant results of their nineteenth-century successors. There is only one wood engraver of any importance, therefore, in the eighteenth century: Jean-Michel Papillon. The whole art of wood engraving was summed up in him; whenever a fine typographical ornament was wanted, it was Papillon who was approached for it.

WILLIAM HOGARTH. *The Company of Undertakers*

Papillon (1698-1776) belonged to a family of wood engravers who had worked throughout the seventeenth century, making funeral invitations and wall-papers. He was more of an artist than the rest of them, in addition, he was a theorist and an historian, and his *Histoire de la gravure sur bois* (1766) is still well-known and extremely useful, since it gives a great many names otherwise unknown (he began working on it in 1734).

Papillon decided very early that he wanted to be an artist. When he was nine, he began to engrave on wood copies of works by Callot and Israël Silvestre, though he had to do it surreptitiously, because the only kind of work his father acknowledged was wall-paper designing. His work was soon noticed and its quality recognized amid the general decadence of the woodcut, and from 1713, when he was only sixteen, he began to receive numerous commissions from the Paris book trade. He engraved armorial bearings, fleurons, and tail-pieces, with little figures and decorative subjects pleasing in design and quite well drawn. He was so devoted to his work that he wore himself out at it; his sight was affected by its minute and detailed character. He was at it night and day, to such an extent that his wife became anxious; she never saw anything of him, and thought that he was neglecting her for a mistress: 'I found her in tears one day, but I reassured her.' He was highly esteemed among publishers, and by other illustrators as well, even the designers of copper-plate vignettes. Choffard asked him for some of his blocks, in order to examine them, and told Papillon that he was very much struck by the beauty of their execution—this was clearly a great compliment.

He went on working till about 1756, then presented his *œuvre* to the Cabinet des Estampes, where he had long been a frequent visitor in search of ideas for his designs. But by this time, and more especially in 1762, as we shall now see, a new kind of work was being tried outside France.

WILLIAM HOGARTH. *The Rake's Progress,* V: *He Marries an Old Maid*

WILLIAM HOGARTH

The first important figure we encounter outside France is the Englishman William Hogarth. When he died in 1764, he left all his property to his wife; it consisted chiefly of 'plates engraved on copper', which can be regarded as symbolic, since in spite of a few outstanding successes in painting, Hogarth the engraver far surpasses Hogarth the painter. In any case, he had always wanted to engrave. 'Engraving on copper', he declared, 'was, at twenty years of age, my utmost ambition.' From early childhood (he was born in London in 1697) he was passionately devoted to drawing, preferring it to any other occupation — 'even to more amusing occupations', his friends used to say. He began by engraving coats-of-arms on silver-plate, then, when he was twenty-three, he engraved his own trade card: 'William Hogarth engraver, April 1720'. Although he was interested in painting for the sake of the social status it could bestow, he turned more readily to engraving, not only because of the natural predilection we have already mentioned, but also because he wished his work to point a moral, and prints could reach a far wider public than he could hope to influence with his paintings. In 1735 he produced the *Rake's Progress,* in 1736 *The Distressed Poet,* in 1738 *Morning, Noon, Night and Evening,* in 1741 *The Enraged Musician,* in 1745 *Marriage à la mode,* and in 1747 *Industry and Idleness.*

Although the opposite has sometimes been argued, the first thing that strikes us about Hogarth's work is not its aesthetic quality, but its literary and moralising aspect: 'One thinks first of the subject', writes Elie Faure, and adds: '... and if there happens to be a fine bit of painting, on the canvas, one only notices it after having enjoyed a good laugh.' What is true of Hogarth's painting is even truer of this prints, which in any case are often only reproductions of works he had already executed on canvas. Hogarth is of the same opinion: 'However difficult it may be, the execution is only of secondary importance, and the artist is aiming at praise of a higher order.' But he also specifies the moral aim of his prints; his desire is to edify as well as to amuse. Hogarth was not a religious man, and still less was he a mystic; he was conventional Englishman whose sense of practical morality was shocked by the dissolute habits of his time. Not without a touch of vanity, he believed himself to be charged with an 'apostolic mission', and he devoted his talent as an engraver to the teaching of moral lessons. His prints set out to attack all the abuses and irregularities he hated, by making them seem ridiculous or detestable. Thus the *A Harlot's Progress,* the *Rake's Progress, Before* and *After* are all satires on debauchery. In plate 6 of the *Rake's Progress* Hogarth also condemns gambling: Thomas Rakewell, the hero, is sent to prison after having dissipated his wife's fortune in a Covent Garden gambling-hell. *Gin Lane* and the *Midnight Modern Conversation* are a vigorously realistic attack on drunkenness, and the four *Election* scenes denounce political venality.

Hogarth also produced social satires, as well as moral ones. These were not directed against any particular social class; he exposes the faults of every class and condemns them all. In *Marriage à la mode* he attacks the loose living of the aristocracy; in *The Bench* and *The Consultation of Physicians* he reproaches the educated middle classes for not practising their professions conscientiously. The four magistrates in *The Bench* are all dozing under their wigs, instead of judging; and the doctors in the *Consultation* are contemplating a urinal with an air of great stupidity.

Struggling artists unable to escape from their wretched lot *(The Enraged Musician,* for example, and *The Distressed Poet)* are no better treated – Hogarth believed that every man can and must succeed by this own efforts. He was himself a living example of the truth of this theory, and, to prove it, he produced the series of prints entitled *Industry and Idleness.* It tells the story of two apprentices who both begin in the same way but end their lives in a very different fashion. One, by dint of hard work and perseverance, wins his master's confidence, marries his daughter, and becomes sheriff and finally Lord Mayor of London; the other, a lazy, careless good-for-nothing, finishes on the gallows for murdering with intent to rob. All are over-simplified representations of a kind which were to reappear in about 1860 in the popular prints produced at Epinal.

Certain practices and certain categories of persons served as targets for Hogarth's personal gibes. He had no respect whatever for the clergy, for example. In all his riotous gatherings a clergyman appears; one is present at the election feast (plate 1 of the *Election* series), another is to be found in squalid and poverty-stricken surroundings (The *Harlot's Progess),* and another in the tavern in the *Midnight Modern Conversation, Credulity, Superstition and Fanaticism, The Sleeping Congregation,* and *Some Inhabitants of the Moon.* All are specific attacks on the clergy.

Hogarth shows himself equally hostile to the soldiery, whether English *(The March to Finchley)* or, still worse from his point of view, the French. His natural antipathy for England's nearest neighbours, which a very short stay in Calais only served to increase, found violent expression in the *Roast Beef of Old England,* and *The Invasion* (where a French officer is depicted as an eater of frogs).

He does not spare his own countrymen, some of whose inclinations, such as cock-fighting, or the collection of oriental art he deplores. He regarded this predilection for *chinoiseries* as the sign of a complete lack of taste; he alludes to it in *Marriage à la mode* (plates 2 and 4), and ridicules it specifically in the plate entitled *Taste in High Life.*

Such, briefly, are the main themes on which Hogarth's satires are based. In order to decide whether he succeeded in resolving the difficult problem of reconciling the demands of art and his passion for satire and moralising, we must study his method of composition, and of engraving.

WILLIAM HOGARTH. *A Harlot's Progress,* I: *Her arrival in London*

WILLIAM HOGARTH. *Beer Street*

Hogarth followed at least three different procedures in composing his works. The first consisted in developing the satire throughout a series or 'suite' of from four to eight engravings; he adopted this system for the *Harlot's Progress,* the *Rake's Progress,* etc. In this case he was using engraving as an equivalent, or even a rival, of the theatre: 'I have endeavoured to treat my subjects as a dramatic writer: my picture is my stage, and men and women my players, who by means of certain actions and gestures, are to exhibit a dumb show.' Hogarth directed this 'dumb show' with implacable logic. When the curtain rises (with the first plate) we are introduced to the principal actor; the second scene reveals – if we are not already aware of them – the vices which will inevitably lead to the hero's final downfall. The epilogue of these 'plays written with a paint-brush', as Walpole calls them, always points a moral, as a fable does. Vice is always punished; Hogarth is unmoved by its attractions, incapable of flattering it even for a moment, entirely preoccupied with catching its precise grimaces and gestures in pleasure or suffering. Driven by an excessive moral necessity Hogarth's satire-dramas unfold in a systematic and monotonous fashion. They lack intrigue; they are without any element of surprise. Hogarth over-simplifies his characters to the point where they are totally good or totally bad. The result of this is a lack of psychological depth. The dramatic action also suffers; the characters experience no inner conflict; there is no struggle, no choice between vice and virtue; having fallen, they take pleasure in their own downfall. We are watching the advance of evil; Hogarth makes it inevitable.

Sometimes he has recourse to another method of working: contrasted pairs of engravings, such as *Gin Lane* and *Beer Street, France* and *England,* or *Before* and *After.* Here there is no series of episodes; Hogarth strikes a couple of blows, and produces an immediate effect. Finally, he often concentrates the satire in a single image: *Taste in High Life,* for example, *The Bench* and *Southwark Fair.*

Whatever method of attack he chooses, Hogarth makes use of all the details in the picture to underline the central theme. His positive nature has no time for abstractions. At the risk of over-emphasis, therefore, he multiplies details which express his thoughts in a concrete and explicit fashion. Everything is symbolic, imaginative, even the names: the industrious apprentice of *Industry and Idleness* is called Frank

Goodchild, while the lazy one's name is Thomas Idle. Nothing is left in doubt. The 'distressed poet' is living in a miserable garret, he holds a pen in his hand, and he has just written *Riches, a poem.* Behind him, on the wall, is a plan of the silver mines in Peru. The cupboards are empty. The poet's wife sits patching clothes in the middle of the room. Their child is crying; he is cold and hungry. The door is open, and a woman has come to demand money... Unlike the Japanese engravers and draughtsmen, who can suggest an idea in a line, convey it with precision and the utmost economy, Hogarth expresses himself in a diffuse and verbose fashion. He does not select the pose, the gesture, the word which sums up and explains the whole situation. In this sense, his style is more literary than graphic. But, as M. Paul Prouté has said, 'there is an intense life animating this work; it seems about to leave its frame as we look at it, and evolve as a real life drama in front of our very eyes—anticipating, in fact, the art of the cinema'.

However, although Hogarth evidently worked out the composition of his engravings conscientiously and with the utmost care, their execution seems uneven, if not actually careless. They were done on a large scale, so that they could be hung on a wall and would be easy to 'read' at a distance, and the quality of the engraved line is hard and intensive. Hogarth was aware of this, but believed that it was suited to the moral purpose of this work: 'The passions may be more forcibly expressed by a strong bold stroke, than by the most delicate engraving. To expressing them as I felt them, I have paid the utmost attention, and as they were addressed to hard hearts, have rather preferred leaving them hard, and giving the effect, by a quick touch, to rendering them languid and feeble by fine strokes and soft engraving.' We must therefore accept his rigidity of style as deliberate. But Hogarth also wished his prints to be cheap and popular; referring to *The Four Stages of Cruelty,* he writes: 'The leading points in these, as well as the two preceding prints, were made as obvious as possible, in the hope that their tendency might be seen by men of the lowest rank. Neither minute accuracy of design, nor fine engraving, was deemed necessary, as the latter would render them too expensive for the persons to whom they were intended to be useful.'

Hogarth's original and precise intention to use his engravings for the instruction of all and sundry, and not merely for the amusement of a

WILLIAM HOGARTH. *First Stage of Cruelty*

few privileged members of society, explains why he was to some extent unconcerned with their aesthetic qualities; it also accounts for the very moderate prices at which he sold them. However, his idealistic generosity did not entail the sacrifice of commercial interests; he devoted much attention to organizing the production and sale of his prints, and to protecting them from pirated copies, of which there were a great number. He had already suffered from this practice in 1728: 'The first plate I published', he tells us, 'called *The Taste of the Town* (i.e. *Masquerades and Operas),* in which the reigning follies were lashed, had no sooner begun to take a run, than I found copies of it in the print-shops, vending at half-price, while the original prints were returned to me again.'

In 1735, he presented a petition to Parliament requesting that the right of ownership of engravers over their own works should be protected, and that it should be forbidden to make reproductions of these without the artist's consent. '...After having had my plates pirated in almost all sizes, I in 1735 applied to Parliament for redress, and obtained it in so liberal a manner, as hath not only answered my own purpose, but made prints a considerable article in the commerce of this country; there being now more business of this kind done here, than in Paris, or anywhere else, and as well.' However, in spite of this law and Hogarth's statements, the plagiarists reappeared on the scene, and Hogarth suffered from them again on many occasions. Perhaps it was this constant pirating that persuaded him to employ assistants; he had a large number of engravers in his pay, including several Frenchmen who had settled in London. Bernard Baron (1696-1762/6), Louis-Gérard Scotin (1690-after 1755) and Simon-François Ravenet (1706-1774) all worked for the well-known publisher Boydell, and engraved prints after Hogarth's drawings or paintings—in particular, *Marriage à la mode.* Hogarth also employed artists of French descent such as Charles Grignion (born in London 1716, died 1810) and François Morellon La Cave (born in Amsterdam), and, of course, English engravers, including Charles Mosley (1720-1770), William Woolet (1735-1785), Thomas Major (1714-1720/99), James Basire (1730-1802), and Luke Sullivan (born in Ireland in 1705, died in London in 1771).

Sometimes Hogarth entrusted the entire execution of a plate to these professional engravers (who were fully qualified and well-known artists, some of them belonging to the Society of Artists or members of the Royal Academy), sometimes the task was shared, and he and his assistants collaborated on the same plate. None of the engravings shows any individuality of talent, and, except perhaps for *Beer Street, Gin Lane* and *The Four Stages of Cruelty,* published under Hogarth's direction but not bearing the engraver's name (it was probably Hogarth himself), all the plates from his studio have the same characteristics—careful execution, monotony, and insensitiveness. Yet they are of better quality, and engraved with less dullness, than the copies published by Bowles (cf. the *Midnight Modern Conversation* and the *Harlot's Progress),* and they are certainly more in the spirit of Hogarth than the mezzotints by Spooner, or the mezzotint reproductions in green ink by Elisha Kirkall (1682-1742), both of which present an entirely different appearance because of the process employed.

The fact that pirated copies were produced in such quantities is enough to prove the success of Hogarth's engravings—at least from the popular and commercial point of view. They were less appreciated on the artistic plane (such, after all, was not his intention). The painter-engraver Chodowiecki, who was also a collector and particularly fond of French drawings, writes from Berlin in 1779: 'My pleasure in the composition, the invention and the poetry of Hogarth's works is equalled by my dissatisfaction with his drawing and execution...' On the other hand numerous witnesses testify to their success in teaching a moral lesson. Fielding, who was full of admiration for him, claimed that he was the most useful satirist who had ever lived, and that the *Rake's Progress* and the *Harlot's Progress* served the cause of virtue far better than any amount of weighty volumes full of moral treatises. He even declared that a respectable household should no more be without these two sets of prints than without *The Whole Duty of Man.* John Clubbe, in the foreword to his *Physiognomy,* also expresses his conviction that Hogarth's works must have saved many from ruin, and that they served as a warning which was remembered long after the rigid teachings of dogmatism had been rejected or forgotten. The *Physiognomy,* published in London in 1763, was announced as the simple outline of a larger work on the same subject, in which the different temperaments, passions and habits of men were examined in detail.

In the province of art history, Hogarth's essential merit was in giving both English painting and English engraving a national character. He was of an independent nature, and fought violently against foreign importations and what he called the blind worship of ancient works. He defended the art of his contemporaries, and denounced the patina acquired through age. Time, he declared, ruined the harmony of colours, turning them all brown (see his engraving *Time smoking pictures,* 1761). He refused to learn from the work of French, Italian, German and Dutch artists *(Paul before Felix, designed and etched in the ridiculous manner of Rembrandt),* and stoutly defended his views, claiming that his principles were all founded on nature, and that he did not depart from nature and from truth. Hogarth came to be appreciated not only in London but on the continent as well. In Rouquet's *Letters* on the state of the arts in England (1755, second French edition dedicated to Marigny), the author stresses the importance of Hogarth. Diderot also knew Hogarth; in about 1780 people still 'snatched Hogarth's prints from one another's hands, and the head of every family felt obliged to buy them'. And in Germany Hogarth's success dates from 1794, as Antal has shown.

It is to Hogarth's successful revolt against conformity that English engraving, hitherto a mediocre and insignificant offshoot of French and Flemish schools, owes its sudden rapid progress. Hogarth is the father of English caricature, of which Rowlandson and Gillray were to be the great names; but before we meet the latter, at the end of the eighteenth century, we must study the Italian etchers, who were already revolutionizing the aesthetics of print-making in Hogarth's own day.

Thirty-four engravings which Canaletto executed in Venice between 1740 and 1743 were to have a profound influence on the century. Thirty-one of them went to make up the volume entitled *Vedute altre prese da i luoghi, altre ideate, da Antonio Canal...* ('Views, some after nature, some imaginary, by Antonio Canal, engraved and drawn in perspective by himself, humbly presented to the most illustrious Signor Joseph Smith, Consul of His Britannic Majesty, as a token of esteem and respect'.) The other three are landscapes of which only a single proof is known.

Canaletto, then more than forty years old, was born in 1697 to a noble Venetian family. His father was also an artist and a designer for the theatre, but Canaletto abandoned theatre work in 1719 and devoted himself to painting views. He remained in Venice till about 1746, then went on his travels, paying several very successful visits to England. He died in Venice in 1768, leaving a considerable body of paintings. Most of his patrons were English, introduced to him through the good offices of Joseph Smith, the British Consul in Venice, who was a collector, scholar and dealer. Some of Smith's biographers show him as a faithful friend, others as a shrewd business man. In any case, he certainly gave Canaletto his support, and, as the dedication just quoted shows, we are indebted to him for the publication of the artist's engraved work.

Although these *vedute* are not dated, Canaletto probably executed his engravings between 1740 and 1750; more exactly, between 1740 and 1743. The series of etchings must have been published after 1740, the year in which Smith was appointed Consul, since the dedication mentions this appointment. In addition, the imaginary view of Venice usually known as *The House with the Inscription* is inscribed with the date of its execution, 1741. Moreover, Palluchini has pointed out that the study for the 'view of a village by a river' dates from 1742.

With the aid of these valuable landmarks, and given the fact that the execution of the series is so coherent in style that it does not seem possible for it to have been spread over many years, it is reasonable to suppose that Canaletto's engraving was done between 1740 and 1743 – a 'pause for reflection', in the apt phrase of Palluchini, at the peak of his artistic maturity.

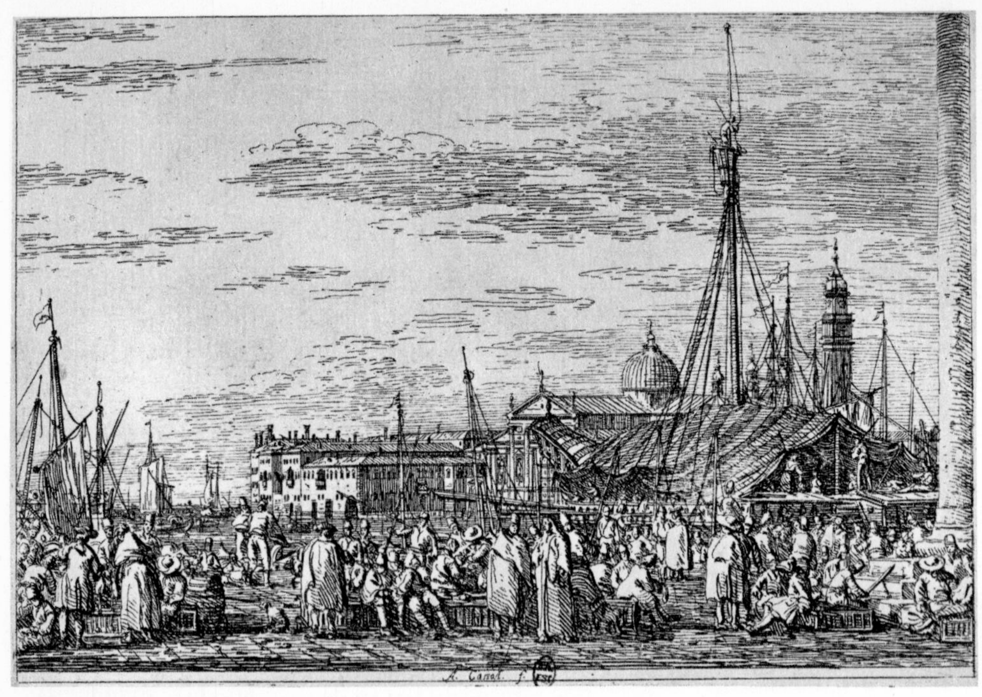

ANTONIO CANALETTO. *The Market in the Piazzetta, Venice*

We do not know in what order the thirty-one engravings originally appeared in Smith's collection. However, Meyer, and later Frietzsche and Palluchini, have attempted to establish it, and seem to have got somewhere near the original order; we will therefore follow Palluchini's numbering.

On the title page, Canaletto announces that some of the views he offers us are from nature, and others imaginary. The two categories are clearly distinguished on the prints themselves, since the actual views (seven large and four small) have a title in the lower margin, and the others have none. But whether the scenes are real or invented, the subject is always Venice (from Venice itself as far as Padua, along the banks of the Brenta). However, it is not the courtly Venice that Canaletto shows us here—the capital of the Doges, sumptuously decked, richly adorned for some solemn pilgrimage or some important festival (as we see her in his painting of *The Bucentaur before the Ducal Palace on Ascension Eve,* or *The Doge's Pilgrimage to the Church of St Nicholas)*—but the inner Venice, homely, vital, unadorned. To evoke this everyday Venice, busy and industrious, Canaletto laid aside the paint-brush, and expressed all her poetry with his etching-needle.

And, indeed, once he leaves the Piazza San Marco and the Piazzetta (all too familiar places, which he still engraves too stiffly), even his most faithful views become intimate little poems, luminous and tender; the *Porte del Dolo,* for example (where, in an intense depth of shadow which does not deny the light but rather seems to glorify it, a shallop leaves

ANTONIO CANALETTO. *Torre di Malghera*

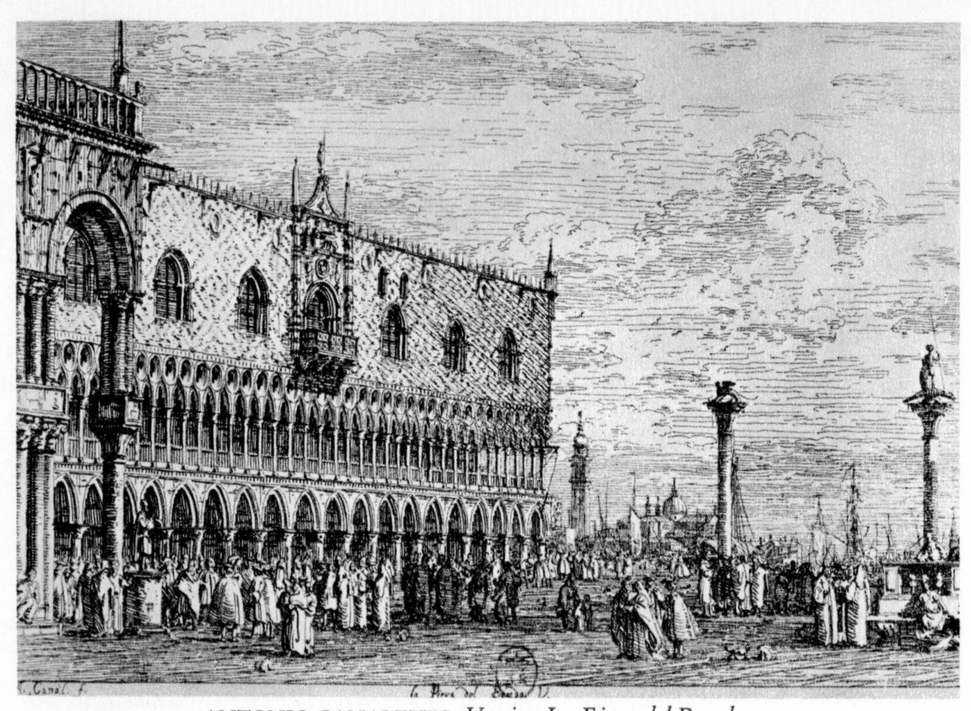

ANTONIO CANALETTO. *Venice: La Fiera del Bando*

the locks and makes its way towards the lagoon), *al Dolo, San Cristina in Pra della valle,* and above all *La Torre di Malghera* in its desolate and neglected surroundings. While practical in his approach to this medium, Canaletto lends a magic to his scenes, 'dusting them with a shimmer of light... Light and shadow, half-lights and reflections interact and multiply in joyous exuberances'. (Palluchini, p. 14.)

The imaginary places of his dreams are equally poetic. His fanciful reconstructions of districts in Venice are arranged with such naturalness that they radiate all the charm of that city, as, for example, *The Terrace,* or the landscape with a pilgrim praying at a cross-roads, the view of a meadow with a woman drawing water at a well beneath an arch, or the tranquil scene with a boat drifting silently with the flow of the water.

Unlike his predecessors (Carlevarijs, Ricci and Marieschi), Canaletto

ANTONIO CANALETTO. *Portico with a Lantern*

seems to be unconcerned with providing documentary information. Carlevarijs had inaugurated the Venetian tradition of 'views' in 1703, but his etchings (there are a hundred and four of them) are overladen with detail, and his execution is 'painstaking, dull, and without any element of surprise'. Marco Ricci's twenty landscapes were published in 1730, after his death, and the twenty-one etchings by Marieschi came out in Venice in 1741 (see Mme Pittaluga). Canaletto left 'the sights of Venice' to them, and set out to show us his dream—the Venice he saw and knew, and not Venice as the tourists saw her. He had not the decorator's approach, like his contemporary Tiepolo. His choice of subjects reveals the quality of his vision—sensitive and pure, with a kind of innocence of eye which enabled him to find beauty in the humblest landscape. There is nothing grand or imposing, nothing extraordinary or monumental in his prints; nothing is exaggerated, sham, or contrived. There is a delightful humanity about the beauty of this withdrawn Venice, intimate and without artifice, and about the atmosphere surrounding her. Only a Venetian of extraordinary perception would have chosen to reveal her to us, and only an exceptionally gifted artist could have expressed, through the medium of engraving, such a combination of ideal harmony and truth to nature.

ANTONIO CANALETTO. *The Prison, Venice*

Canaletto was clearly not in the least restricted by his medium. His etching-needle moves freely over the copper creating the most delicate nuances by smooth undulating lines or by faint and broken strokes. Sometimes the power of his drawing, with its reiteration of short, agitated strokes, is so striking that 'by analogy one cannot help thinking of what Van Gogh was to achieve, two centuries later, with obsessively repeated lines.' (Palluchini, p. 19.)

Canaletto arranges the elements of his composition with great skill. Thus, to give a panoramic effect to *Pra della Valle,* he makes the town square extend towards the upper part of the picture. Elsewhere, he gives depth to his picture by means of a varied interplay of shade and light—light, direct or reflected, penetrating or diffused, which gives his etchings their balanced harmony and their sparkling life. Moreover, in his concern not so much for the light itself as for the reaction of various objects—stones, water, foliage—to light, Canaletto sometimes seems to have an 'impressionist' feeling for landscape.

No inferior detail mars these vibrant and beautifully composed works. Canaletto's figures fit naturally into the landscape they animate. Attempts have been made to attribute them to Tiepolo, but they are too consistent in style and spirit to have been a subsequent addition. The architectural elements are correctly drawn, but never spoilt by overmuch precision.

Unfortunately, one looks in vain for this delicacy and expressiveness in the work of Gianfrancesco Costa *(Delle delizie del fiume Brenta, espresse nei Palazzi e casini situati sopra sue sponde della sua sboccatura nella lazuna di Venezia fino alla citta di Pavoda...,* 1747-56, two volumes, 170 plates), a meticulously factual set of views of a more strictly tourist itinerary. A glance at Costa's *Al dolo* is enough to show how Canaletto's etchings have, as it were, been 'drained of their substance'. Costa is not master of his craft; his strokes are often clumsy, and lack flexibility. Anxious to 'put some life' into his pictures, and at the same time lacking any sense of poetry, he invents all kinds of sham episodes: gondolas accidentally collide, a storm blows up, an extraordinary smoke blackens the sky. There is none of this in Canaletto, no unwarranted episodes or irregular happenings. Moreover, Costa's figures, unlike those of Canaletto, do not seem to belong to their setting; they 'pose' and distract our attention by anecdote and 'picturesque' detail.

Canaletto's etchings probably had a greater influence on his nephew, Bernardo Bellotto, than on Costa. Bernardo was the son of Canaletto's elder sister; he was his uncle's pupil for several years, and out of the thirty-seven plates which make up his engraved *œuvre,* the first eight, executed in Italy, are in the same style as Canaletto's small views. The large views of cities, however, composed later when he was in Saxony and Poland, have entirely lost the graceful serenity and intimacy of Canaletto's little imaginary landscapes.

Another interpreter of the Venetian scene, Francesco Guardi, was influenced by Canaletto's etchings, though he never did any engraving

GIOVANNI BATTISTA TIEPOLO. *Adoration of the Magi*

himself. He took over some of the themes directly into his paintings, such as *La Piera del Bando V, La Biblioteca V, The walk on the Mole.* (Palluchini, p. 26.) But the relationship between these two artists does not go very deep. Guardi's nervous abbreviations and fantastic evocations are foreign to Canaletto. Moreover, in spite of occasional echoes in the work of a few artists, Canaletto's prints remain a thing apart, a unique and very personal manifestation of his art. They are rare and precious, free and luminous. They guide us through a Venice less urbane, more endearing and in a way more 'authentic' than the Venice in his paintings, and constitute one of the most intimate and poetic pages in the history of eighteenth-century art.

In 1749, a suite of engravings was published in Venice which, like the preceding ones, was to achieve considerable fame: the *Capricci* of Giovanni Battista Tiepolo.

Tiepolo was at this time fifty-three years old, and was at the summit of his brilliant career as a decorative painter. In the following year he was to leave Venice for Wurtzburg, then for Madrid, where he died suddenly in 1770. Engraving was never an activity of any importance for him; his prints are limited in number; Sack's catalogue (the most complete) only contains thirty-eight items. But in spite of this, Tiepolo is one of the great masters of the print, and one of those whose work has a particularly individual character.

His total output consists of two series of plates. The first was the *Capricci*—ten etchings (he never used any other process), oblong in shape, first published in Venice by Anton Maria Zanetti in his collection entitled *Raccolta di varie stampe a chiaroscuro tratte dei disegni originali di Fr. Massuoli... e altri insigni autori.* The proofs from this first addition are not numbered or signed. Tiepolo's second series of prints, the *Scherzi di fantasia,* were engraved later, and only appeared after his death, in 1775. They were published by the artist's eldest son, Domenico, who added engravings by himself and by his brother Lorenzo. To this series of twenty-three undated plates (twenty-one upright and two of landscape format) have been added two plates of religious subjects: *St Joseph carrying the Holy Child,* and an *Adoration of the Magi,* which served as a title page, and which (because of a mistake of Cean Bermudez) has wrongly been taken for a reproduction of a painting by the artist at San Pascual d'Aranjuez.

To these two series, one can perhaps add two small plates featuring magicians, described and reproduced by Sack, and possibly a third with studies of heads and trophies, signed Tiepolo-Algarotti.

The two series of etchings are not identical in spirit. The ten small plates of the *Capricci* (a title in vogue, but somewhat imprecise, since Piranesi was able to apply it to his *Carceri* series and Goya to his visions and his bitter imaginings) are remarkable for the brilliance of their imaginative power. There is no precise theme running through them; the setting and characters, however, are always the same—women, children and soldiers gather in groups of three or four and converse together. It is impossible to guess the subject of their inaudible discussions; sometimes they seem to be questioning one another, and bend forward to speak softly—yet what have they to fear? A voice does not carry so far among those ruins. There is a strange air of mystery about them. Almost all the elements of the *Scherzi* are already present in the *Capricci*. There are peaceful, everyday scenes among them; a child, reclining, writes on the ground with a finger, or plays with pebbles, and his action is natural and unforced (Hind, 3). A strikingly beautiful woman (Hind, 6), with a very upright carriage, pauses in her work; she rests her arms on an urn, and talks with two seated soldiers. A cavalier prepares to mount his horse (Hind, 12). A woman drowses in the open air (Hind, 7).

Everywhere, there is a hint of witchcraft, in the disturbing way the sage stares at the shoulder of the young warrior who has risen to leave, his hand on his shield (Hind 11), in the sleeping woman on whose breast there leans, not a child, but a satyr (Hind 7). Death and magic were later to be the two closely interwoven themes of the *Scherzi,* but allusions to death already appear in the plates of the *Capricci*: in one, a woman with bound hands is gazing at a serpent and some bones (Hind, 9); elsewhere Death himself dictates his decrees in the presence of a group of characters among whom even the magician appears uneasy (Hind, 10). Tiepolo's *Capricci* led him to the vision of death; his 'exercises of imagination' took him no further, for henceforth death figures constantly.

The *Scherzi* always have an open-air setting, but it is still vague and indeterminate. On the ground lie again the trophies, shields, and traces of forgotten bas-reliefs, but a new and macabre element is introduced:

GIOVANNI BATTISTA TIEPOLO. *The Tomb of Punchinello*

GIOVANNI BATTISTA TIEPOLO. *Capriccio*

human bones and skulls. A strange menagerie serves to increase the disquieting atmosphere of these places dedicated to some obscure and evil cult; on each plate, a serpent writhes on the ground, or twists itself round a stick. On the rare occasions when the serpent is absent, an owl accompanies the magician; sometimes it remains at a distance, perched on a branch, sometimes it lies, crouching beside the turbanned priest (Hind, 20). Other animals are introduced—a monkey, a dog, some sheep—but only the owl and the serpent share in the mysteries, for there can be no doubt that the magician of the *Capricci,* grown old and gnarled (and wrongly believed to be descended from Rembrandt's

GIOVANNI BATTISTA TIEPOLO. *Man with a Horse*

Philosopher) has just presided over strange mysteries, or is conducting some initiation ceremony among young children (Hind, 25, 26, 34). Without the intervention of the magician, four of the plates from the *Scherzi* (Hind, 27, 28, 31 and 33) would recall some familiar scene from the *Capricci.* But his presence changes the whole atmosphere. Where it was calm and sunny, it has become dark and ominous. At his approach, faces turn away and eyes are averted (Hind, 27 and 28).

One of the most saddening of the *Scherzi* is the plate (Hind, 30) showing the magician crouching to play joylessly with a monkey, beside a man lost in mournful thoughts; one of the most ambiguous shows the old sage pretending to philosophize (Hind, 32), when he is more probably a sorcerer plotting some new evil, some spell to cast. The most Venetian in character are those where we meet Punchinello (Hind, 21 and 29) or his rediscovered corpse.

However strange the *Scherzi* may seem to us, they do not appear to be quite so original a creation when we realize the importance of magic in eighteenth-century Italy. The Age of Enlightenment did not scorn such foolishness; all Italy (and decadent Venice was particularly vulnerable) involved itself in it to such an extent that Maffei found it necessary to write several books against this new scourge – magic. The *Scherzi* therefore represent a very real aspect of the intellectual life of Venice at this time.

However, although *Capricci* may seem enigmatic and mysterious in conception, and the *Scherzi* even more so, they are clear and simple in expression, just as Tiepolo's handwriting is perfectly and immediately legible. For two centuries, Italian etching had made good progress artistically, in particular Ribera, Salvator Rosa, Della Bella and Castiglione had given it a great deal of freedom. Tiepolo liberates it still further; above all, he bestows on it his own personal qualities of light and 'rapidity'. He makes use of the single stroke – that is, without crossed lines. Just as, in painting, he abandons sombre colours, so also his etching-needle seeks out delicate harmonies, and not strong contrasts. It does not plough into the copper but skims over it. It caresses the surface, without penetrating deeply. Thus, with short, free strokes, broken and varied, he produces etchings exquisitely silvery and luminous in quality.

Tiepolo's first disciples were, naturally, his own sons. Gian Domenico, the eldest of seven (1727-1795), left a considerable body of work (177 plates), some reproducing his father's pictures and some designed by himself. We have only nine plates by Lorenzo, all after his father's compositions, and revealing a genuine talent. The brothers separated after their father's death; the first went back to Venice, pursuing a brilliant career; the second remained in Madrid and was less successful.

Tiepolo is the dominating figure of his century. Without him, those two great artists Fragonard and Goya would probably not have found complete expression. Fragonard did not know him personally, he did not meet him in Venice, but, when he returned from his first Italian

GIOVANNI BATTISTA TIEPOLO. *Flight into Egypt*

journey, the French artist engraved two plates after works by Tiepolo: the *Virgin in Glory* (a free interpretation of the painting in the Gesuati in Venice) and the *Warrior before a tribunal* (which M. G. Wildenstein rightly identifies with the *Mucius Scaevola,* painted for the patriarch Dolfin). But the memory of Tiepolo is even more evident in Fragonard's original prints than in these reproductive engravings.

The same is true of Goya's early plates, such as *Saint Anthony in prayer,* and even of the *Caprichos.* We must repeat, however, that there is nothing tragic about Tiepolo; the ruins, the satyrs, the grimaces, are always in his eyes picturesque and 'fabulous'. His mysterious allegories may surprise, but not frighten us. Even at his most mysterious, he retains his concern for elegant poses; in the *Caprici,* Death is seen from the back, bent in the artist's favourite attitude, because he has a marked preference for the position which best reveals the elegance and suppleness of the human body (Hind, 6, 11, 14, 23, 28). He also bears in mind the importance of balancing opposing elements; in the *Scherzi,* an image of grace and beauty is made to contrast with the ugliness and decrepitude of the sinister magician. Tiepolo is not a visionary, but a lively virtuoso; he is best described as relaxed, light and free, profoundly Italian and Venetian. His prints are bathed in the brilliant light of the Veneto.

In 1745, when Piranesi (1720-1778) was twenty-five, he engraved his *Carceri* in Rome. He sent a copy to Louis XV; and the Directeur des Beaux-Arts, in a letter of thanks to the artist, congratulated him on 'his courage and his fine light effects'. This somewhat terse and clumsy tribute expresses the opinion of a vignettist, used to engraving on a small scale, yet it has pin-pointed Piranesi's chief qualities. It is in fact Piranesi's courage that we admire – a king of fury that makes him attack the copper and produce from it textures and tones often unknown before his time. We also admire his strong chiaroscuro effects – the rays of sunlight and deep shadows so out of keeping with the taste of that day and unknown in that form even among Rembrandt's disciples, yet already heralding the whole romantic movement. But this admiration does not go far enough. Piranesi must be seen, above all, as an outstanding visionary, and one of the great poets of night.

The fourteen plates of his prison scenes, the *Carceri,* revealed his qualities quite early in his career. Prisons were one of the themes of theatrical décor in the eighteenth century; they are to be found in the work of Marot, Bibiena and others. The terror which a prison should inspire was not achieved by representing a narrow dungeon (the stage of an opera house did not lend itself to such a scene) but, on the contrary, by the overpowering immensity of mighty architectural forms, where a man is imprisoned alone, crushed by the sheer mass, which dominates him without any need of chains. The same spirit is present in the *Carceri* which were closely related in theme to contemporary works. The prison scenes of the theatre were also illuminated, and again Piranesi gave similar treatment to his plates. But the public seems to

GIAMBATTISTA PIRANESI. *Prison Scene from the Carceri*

GIAMBATTISTA PIRANESI. *Prison Scene from the Carceri*

have objected, and if we can rely on some information given by his sons, Piranesi refused to listen to criticism, referring the critics to his publisher, Bouchard, who after issuing a small number of *pale* impressions, published the *dark* edition of 1761, which is the one generally known. Piranesi was therefore obliged to please his public, and what we see of his work is probably not entirely due to him. We now know that, contrary to what was formerly believed, the *Carceri* must be judged by the very first printing (nowadays beyond price, and a copy of which Atherton Curtis has presented to the Cabinet des Estampes in Paris). This *pale* printing reveals Piranesi's complete mastery of his craft and altogether modern approach which comes near to that of present-day

GIAMBATTISTA PIRANESI. *Prison Scene from the Carceri*

artists; it must have amazed and shocked even the admirers of Tiepolo and Canaletto. The *Carceri* express the sadness and loneliness of their creator, a man unable to keep his friends, always jealous of his wife, and who was vigorously attacked for his archaeological theories. Our own age, which has also known imprisonment, sorrow and excess, has taken Piranesi to its heart.

Although the *Carceri* remain his masterpiece, one must not forget the thousands of plates he engraved (some earlier than the *Carceri* but the majority later) showing the magnificence of Roman ruins. They are complex works by a man who was on the one hand an architect, archaeologist, and polemicist who conducted press campaigns with their

GIAMBATTISTA PIRANESI. *Rome: the Pantheon*

GIAMBATTISTA PIRANESI. *Rome: the Forum of Nerva*

help, and on the other a fine engraver with a sense of poetry and a most individual and felicitous conception of the arrangement of the elements of his composition. He shows the monuments to their best advantage and, covering them with brambles, shrubs and foliage, softens the harsh outlines of the architecture.

Piranesi's work had an immediate effect, thanks to friends in very differing fields: the sculptor Clérisseau, the painter Vien (both Frenchmen), and the English decorator Robert Adam. His influence was felt in painting, in architectural decoration, and even architecture itself, since Newgate prison was inspired by the *Carceri*. Copies of *Prisons* were distributed to draw attention to the horror of the Bastille dungeons. But it was near 1798 that his influence was strongest; it was strengthened by the summoning of his sons to Paris to establish a school of engraving. Piranesi was even more celebrated in the nineteenth century than in the eighteenth. For us, he is one of the great masters among the painter-engravers.

THE ART OF THE FRENCH PAINTER-ENGRAVERS: FRAGONARD, SAINT-AUBIN AND THE AMATEURS

'Etching', remarked the elder Joullain *fils*, in 1786 (*Réflexions...*, p. 92), 'serves to set down faithfully and with vigour an artist's felicitous ideas'. We are therefore fortunate in possessing a great many etchings by the most outstanding artists, in which talent and the stamp of genius is clearly revealed; etching is 'suited both to the artist and to the amateur inasmuch as it combines facility and rapidity of execution' (*id.*, p. 60). These words throw light on our chapter; in them, an audacious print dealer is expressing ideas which were new at the time. In the eighteenth century, the burin was no longer regarded as the only method of expression; painters and amateur artists, desirous of finding a simpler and quicker procedure, made use of etching to express their 'felicitous ideas'. Times had indeed changed since the seventeenth century, when etching was hardly practised except by Rembrandt, and painters did not usually engrave. We are here in the presence of an almost unique phenomenon: everyone engraved, as Baudelaire was to say of his own contemporaries in 1863, but even the amateur engraving of the eighteenth century was better than that of the nineteenth century, because

GERMAIN DE SAINT-AUBIN. *Butterfly Fantasies: Pyrotechny*

it formed part of the education of a gentleman or a lady of society. Professional artists, as well as amateurs, also tried their hand at it, several of them with considerable distinction.

Let us state, first of all, that this chapter could well be entitled 'From Rembrandt to Rembrandt'. Etching throughout the whole of the eighteenth century is dominated by his influence, though it did not always show itself in the same way, since there are at least two Rembrandts revealed in his engravings: the Rembrandt of *Six's Bridge* and the Rembrandt of the *Hundred Guilder Print*. The first is a rapid, summary draughtsman, who can suggest forms in a few strokes executed in a

GERMAIN DE SAINT-AUBIN. *Butterfly Fantasies: The Tight-rope Walker*

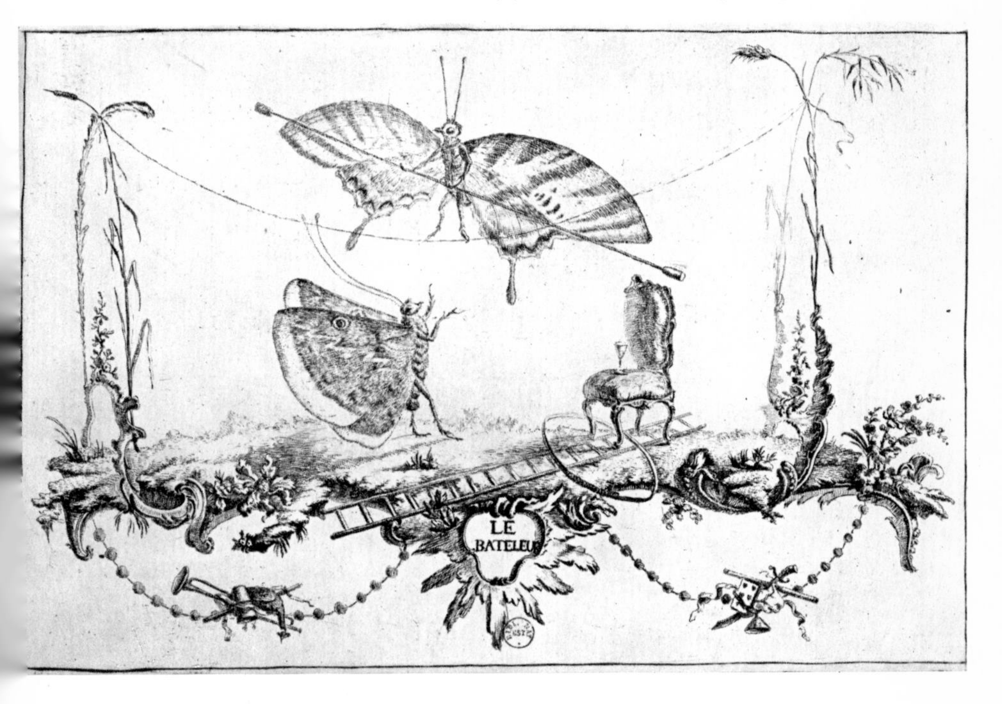

HONORÉ FRAGONARD. *The Swing*. 1782. Engraved by De Launay

HONORÉ FRAGONARD. *The Closet*

couple of minutes (in the time, tradition tells us, that it takes to carry a pot of mustard from one side of a bridge to the other). The Rembrandt of the *Hundred Guilder Print* is a master of chiaroscuro, of elaborately worked effects of light and shadow. Both were to have their effect on French etchers. The *joie de vivre* of the century was to be represented in the lighter style of etching, and the more sombre manner was used in connection with the problems and the great social schemes which were to bring about the Revolution.

The lighter kind of etching was made popular through the influence of painters who has been to Italy and had an opportunity of admiring

HONORÉ FRAGONARD. *La Chemise Enlevée.* 1787. Engraved by Guersant

HONORÉ FRAGONARD. *Satyrs playing*

HONORÉ FRAGONARD. *Bacchanalia*

prints by Tiepolo. Yves Bruand has demonstrated this in an exhibition catalogue which has since become famous, in connection with Coypel, Barrocel, Natoire and Claude. The best of these was Fragonard, who engraved just over thirty plates, of which more than half are reproductive prints. Among the others, apart from those he signed with Mme Gérard, *The Little Park* (about 1763) and the *Bacchanalia* (1763) are enough to ensure him a leading place in the history of original engraving. Probably no other artist has ever engraved with greater spirit; the trees in *The Little Park,* the bas-reliefs in the *Bacchanalia* and the figures in the light

HONORÉ FRAGONARD. *The Stubborn Donkey*
Engraved by Saint-Non

HONORÉ FRAGONARD. *La Culbute.* 1766. Engraved by F. P. Charpentier

in the *Traitants* are all inimitable with their air of simple sketch. In *The Closet* (1778) Fragonard goes further, and this large plate is engraved with more detail, which is perhaps why it is a little heavier.

Gabriel de Saint-Aubin (1724-1780) was another great master of the free style of engraving; he was working a little earlier than Fragonard, in about 1750. Before that, he had been a painter, a pupil of Boucher, and had competed several times unsuccessfully for the Prix de Rome. After 1750, discouraged by his lack of progress, he confined himself to drawing and he was to be found everywhere, whatever the occasion, a pencil in his hand. He drew the whole time, wherever he happened to be—street scenes, entertainments, little everyday happenings, new

HONORÉ FRAGONARD. *Le Chiffre d'Amour.* 1787.
Engraved by De Launay

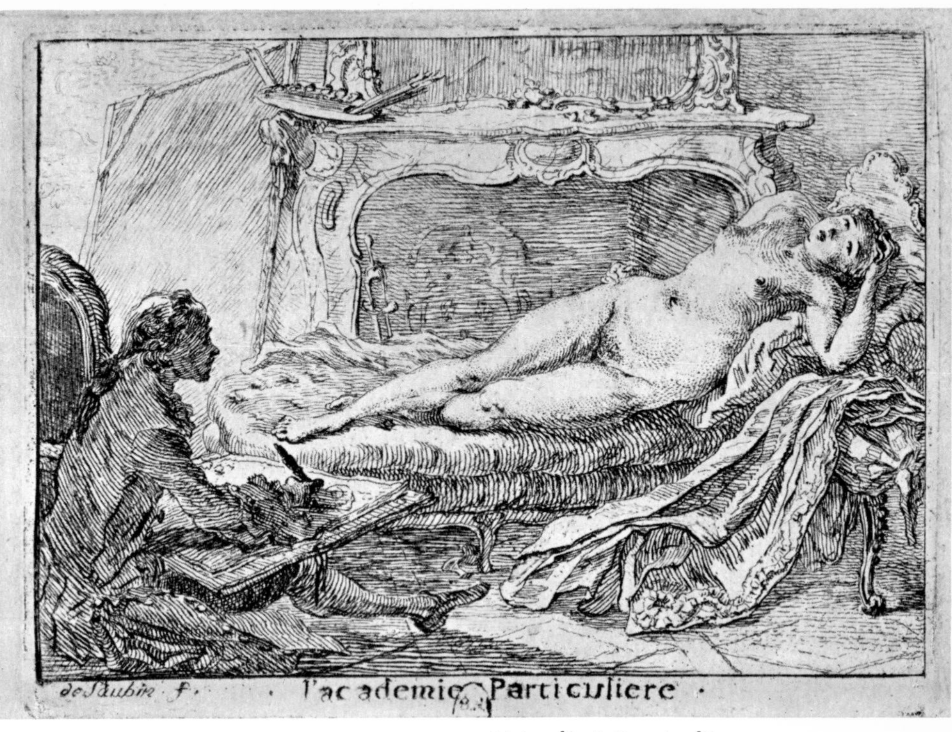

GABRIEL DE SAINT-AUBIN. *L'Académie Particulière*

buildings. To make a living, he specialized in drawings for the margins of Salon catalogues and sale catalogues (which were not illustrated at that period) to serve as reminders of the pictures. He began doing this before 1761; he was mentioned in 1772 and 1779, and earned the title *Croquetel.* His brother, Charles-Germain, pursued the same activity till 1785.

We mention his drawings because his etchings are an extension of them. His total output of engravings consists of about fifty plates, of genre subjects and scenes of contemporary life: *La Foire de Bezons* (1750), *Les Nouvellistes* (1752), *Le Salon du Louvre* (1753), *Les Chaises aux Tuileries* (1760), *L'Académie particulière.* For him, as his historian Dacier so rightly says, 'the copper plate is simply the page of a sketch book, and working on the ground is drawing with the needle. He uses the etching-needle just as he pleases, disregarding rules, and unabashed

AUGUSTIN DE SAINT-AUBIN. *Madame de Pompadour*. 1764.
Engraved after Cochin

HONORÉ FRAGONARD. *The Little Park*

at his daring. It travels over the plate like a pencil. It outlines the features of a composition, enlivens the contours with a few accents, brings out the highlights, blurs the shadows... retraces its steps, adds a few scrawls, and ends by saying exactly what it wants to say.' His prints exist in a number of states—he did not produce them for sale, but continued his researches, producing new states after an interval of years and touching them up with watercolour.

Saint-Aubin is without equal, but he was not the only etcher in his family; it should not be forgotten that among his close relations (fourteen brothers and sisters, of whom six survived childhood) there was a designer of embroidery (his eldest brother, Germain), a painter on porcelain, and two sisters who drew, as well as aunts, nieces, and other relatives. Above all, there was his brother Augustin (1736-1807), his pupil, who from the age of sixteen engraved portraits after Cochin. Cochin was delighted with them, and asserted that he could 'put life

GABRIEL DE SAINT-AUBIN. *Le Salon du Louvre.* 1753

even into the drawing of a wig'. His portrait medallions of intellectuals and cultivated women are his most successful works (1763-1770). (For all the small portraits engraved after Cochin, I would refer the reader to M. Paul Prouté's study.)

Between 1760 and 1770, another etcher was at work who was the quite equal of those previously mentioned. This was the landscape artist Louis Moreau *l'aîné* (1740-1806). His plates have immense charm, and show a feeling for the countryside around Paris which was not to be met with again until the great nineteenth-century masters. The general public would have liked his cottages, his little bridges, his fences among trees and streams, but he only brought them out in one or two series

GABRIEL DE SAINT-AUBIN. *The Procession of the Fatted Ox*

which seem to have been privately issued. They were republished by Naudet in about 1800, when landscape had just been 'discovered' by the pre-romantics.

In addition to these, there were all the amateur engravers. The art was practised by all the keen collectors of prints and drawings, by all the nobility and rich tax-farmers who were interested in the arts, whether by inclination or through snobbery. All these men wanted to engrave, because it was fashionable, and because they saw it being done all around them, but they couldn't manage the burin, so they did etchings under the guidance of the artists they patronised. Never has it been more socially acceptable to take a keen interest in the arts, and to

GABRIEL DE SAINT-AUBIN. *The Two Lovers*

compete with professional artists—amateur artists abounded, and their numbers included women as well as men. The most celebrated of these was Louis XV's mistress, Madame de Pompadour who engraved a series of fifty-two plates after Boucher, reproducing the gems in the Guay collection, and also the very well-known frontispiece to Corneille's *Rodogune,* again after a drawing by Boucher. This was retouched by

GABRIEL DE SAINT-AUBIN. *A Conference of Lawyers*

GABRIEL DE SAINT-AUBIN. *Les Nouvellistes.* 1752

Cochin, and the book was printed in Madame de Pompadour's presence (1760).

Another amateur engraver was M. de Lalive de Jully (1725-1779), the rich *fermier général,* who was an enthusiastic collector and a friend of Mariette; he engraved fifty portraits as a continuation of Perrault's *Hommes Illustres,* helped by Augustin de Saint-Aubin. He was attempting to work in the style of Van Dyck, he tells us, and he presented a set of the plates to Jean-Jacques Rousseau. Claude-Henri Watelet, the Receveur Général, and also a very distinguished amateur, was a member of the French Academy and an honorary member of the Académie des Beaux-Arts. He produced three hundred plates, many of them portrait medallions. The series entitled *Rymbranesques,* 1785, were in imitation of Rembrandt. He died bankrupt in 1786. There was also the Abbé de

LOUIS MOREAU. *The Foot-bridge*

LOUIS MOREAU. *The Cottage*

AUGUSTIN DE SAINT-AUBIN. *At least be discreet!*

AUGUSTIN DE SAINT-AUBIN. *You may count on me!*

MARGUERITE GÉRARD. *The Child and the Bulldog*

Saint-Non, a collector and a friend of Fragonard (*Parc romain* engraved after Fragonard, 1766).

During the following generation, the silvery effect of the *manière blonde* is superseded by richer, deeper tones, as can be seen in the work of Marcenay de Ghuy, Norblin de La Gourdaine, and Boissieu. Marcenay (1724-1811), in his *Idée sur la gravure* (1764), tells us how much he admires Rembrandt. He tries to reproduce the latter's chiaroscuro effects in his *Tobias Recovering his Sight* (1755). Vivant Denon, a brilliant diplomat as well as an enthusiastic amateur, produced numerous etchings in a Rembrandtesque style, although he had learnt his etching

MADAME DE POMPADOUR. *Child*. 1751

NORBLIN DE LA GOURDAINE. *Susannah and the Elders*. 1776

from copying the prints of Callot and Stefano della Bella. Norblin (1745-1830), born near Montereau, worked in Paris and then, in 1774, in Warsaw. He collected Rembrandt's etchings and imitated them. Famous for his knowledge of the techniques of etching, he gave up producing prints in 1789. Bruandet composed very remarkable wild landscapes. The best known of these French etchers is Boissieu, of Lyon (1736-1810), who was influenced by Rembrandt, but even more so by the latter's pupils Lievens and Van Vliet. He was a virtuoso in the medium; his best work was done during the eighteenth century, although Vivant Denon said of his *Little Masons* (1801): 'This print is not only your own *chef-d'œuvre*—it is the greatest masterpiece in the

A. L. DE LALIVE DE JULLY. *Self-portrait. c.* 1760

JEAN-JACQUES DE BOISSIEU. *The Schoolmaster*

history of engraving.' Setting aside this exaggerated praise, Boissieu was indeed a gifted engraver, whose influence was felt by the most important etchers of 1850, Meryon, Bracquemond, and Bléry.

The eighteenth-century painters of this generation, therefore, were trying, as Watteau and his contemporaries had done, to bring about the triumph of their own kind of etching. The general opinion is that they failed to do so, but in my own view the opposite is true. I am, on the contrary, struck by the number of engravers who even tried to imitate etching with the burin. The Academy of Painting and Sculpture in Paris became interested in their work, and Gaucher relates that in about 1750 it instituted an enquiry as to whether it was possible to imitate with the burin the style and the painterly handling of an etching. Nicolas-Gabriel Dupuis (1696-1771) tried to do it; he was originally an etcher, but he had to give up that medium because his health had been injured by the vapours from the acid, which had also affected his eyes. In his engraving *Aeneas saving his father,* therefore, after Carle van Loo, he tried to imitate the characteristics of etching with the burin.

VIVANT DENON. *Breakfast at Ferney.* Engraved by Née and Masquelier

HUBERT ROBERT. *Evening in Rome: The Sarcophagus*

VIVANT DENON. *Self-portrait*

In addition, as we shall see, professional engravers who used the burin engraved their plates over a preparatory etching. Simonet's plates were done over an etched outline by De Launay, others over one by Duclos. The artists who made these preparatory etchings were highly thought of, and few in numbers; when they could not be found in France, they had to be brought from abroad. Daudet, for example, an extremely busy engraver in Paris, sent new copper plates and drawings in 1750 to Hamburg, to have first-class preparatory etchings made by Charles Weisbrodt, who had worked in Paris for ten years.

FRANCE IN THE 'SIXTIES
PROFESSIONAL ENGRAVERS, FIRST ATTEMPTS AT COLOUR, POPULAR PRINTS

We must again turn to France to study the work of the engravers active in about 1760. Although contemporary with Fragonard and Saint-Aubin, their artistic aims were very different from those of the great masters. On the one hand, their style was reminiscent of the beginning of the century and the virtuosi of combined etching and engraving, and on the other, they tried on various levels to abandon black-and-white in favour of colour.

Professional engravers were very numerous. Engraving was a craft which brought in a reasonable income, and was a socially acceptable profession, comparable with that of the present-day photo-engraver. The professional engraver, in fact, spent his life making reproductions of pictures brought to him by private customers, publishers and print-dealers. He engraved them with meticulous care, taking great pride in their perfection, giving them a finish and a brilliance which was much appreciated. The publisher and the engraver were regarded as benefactors of the human race because they made known to the general public works which, before the creation of museums, would without their help, have remained unknown and hidden in private collections. Voltaire states this clearly in *Le Temple du Goût:* 'One Thing God loves even more,' he writes, 'is a collection of prints after the great masters, an enterprise most useful to the human race, which multiplies at little cost the merits of the best painters, which bestows immortality, in all the private collections of Europe, on Beauties which would perish without the help of Engraving, and which can introduce all the schools of painting to a man who has never seen a picture.'

Naturally, these engravers worked together in groups or in studios, and even when their apprenticeship was over, the young men who had come to learn the craft often remained ten years with their master, instead of the statutary four. He gave them full credit in the team-work, and Le Bas, for example, said to his students when he was elected Academician: 'From to-day, gentlemen, you all belong to the Academy.' We know more about Le Bas than about any other head of a studio, thanks to information noted down by Goncourt. We read that 'entry into his house was a promise of talent, the assurance of a successful future. The master did not spare himself, and expected everyone to 'hack away at the copper' as hard as he did, but when the day's work was over he took them all out to enjoy themselves...' Le Bas was particularly fond of engraving Teniers' paintings; there are at least a hundred of them among the 539 plates which constitute his *œuvre.* 'He dedicated his time and his copper to this master whom he would have liked to commemorate, in his enthusiasm, with a mausoleum of marble', but he was also, a little in spite of himself, the populariser of his contemporaries, Chardin, Canot, and Greuze, who entrusted their work to him.

France occupied a central position, and engravers came to study there from all over Europe—England, Germany, Italy, Sweden, and Geneva. John Pine, an English pupil of Bernard Picart, engraved in 1731 a procession of Knights of the Order of the Bath, in the French style. Sir Robert Strange (1721-1792), a Jacobite exile in Paris, returned to London in 1753 but continued to engrave in the French manner; his style was somewhat rigid, his technique a little too perfect. William Wynne Ryland was the pupil of Ravenet in London, and was four years with Le Bas in Paris. Richard Brookshaw, who settled in the rue de Tournon in about 1772, engraved portraits of the future Louis XVI and his wife. Faldoni, born at Arolo in about 1690, learned his engraving in Paris by studying the work of Mellan. A. M. Zanetti (1679-1757) engraved under the direction of Edelinck from 1708. Amigoni, a Viennese, came to Paris in 1736, in between a visit to London and a journey to Spain. Melini (born in 1740) learned to engrave under Beauvarlet. Vangelisti, son of the chancellor of the Florentine legation in Paris, spent a large part of his life working in France, and died there in 1798. Soubeyran, an engraver from Geneva, worked in Paris for twenty years.

Le Bas, Wille and their competitors did a great many engravings of works by contemporary painters, but two of the latter preferred to direct the reproduction of their works themselves. These were Greuze and Chardin, who entrusted the sale of the prints to their wives and had young artists working in their studio among whom they distributed the task of engraving their paintings of genre subjects. Once again, it must be stressed that the sale of an edition of prints brought in twenty or thirty times as much as the sale of a picture. Chardin's genre paintings were nearly all engraved between 1723 and 1757. Mariette, who preferred the grand manner as practised by the history painters, criticised these prints very harshly, emphasising their widespread distribution and deploring it: 'The engravings after M. Chardin's paintings... have now become extremely fashionable, together with those after Teniers, Vauvermans and Lancret, they have succeeded in dealing the final blow to serious prints after Le Brun, Poussin, Le Sueur and even Coypel. The general public takes pleasure in seeing again actions which take place daily under its very eyes in its own home, and unhesitatingly gives them preference over more elevated subjects which require, however, a slight effort to understand...' These engravings were very much sought-after; we read in a comment of 1739 that the public *'se jette sur les estampes de Chardin'.* Copies were made of them, which were known to have sold very cheaply. The press announcement for the sale of the *Dame variant ses amusements,* engraved by Laurent Cars, comes to the defence of Chardin, who does not paint 'pictures which humiliate mankind' like the Flemings do, but is never ugly or disgusting. Lépicié, another interpreter of Chardin's work, engraved *The Grave,* the *Castle of Cards,* and *The Governess.*

Greuze makes a reference to his *commerce* in prints; this artist was associated with four engravers for the reproduction of his pictures – Massard, Gaillard, Levasseur and Flipart. They shared the profits unequally, and Madame Greuze, who ran the business (and was certainly much too interested in the young engravers), thought of all kinds of schemes and subterfuges for making more money – she would print five hundred copies of an engraving when the edition should have consisted of fifty copies, and to increase the profits she invented the system of publishing 'rare states'. She may not have been the first to do this – Chodowiecki, for instance, may have practised it even earlier. She printed several editions of a plate, adding *remarques,* issuing states 'before letters, before the arms, before the dedication, before the publisher's address, before the title of *'peintre du Roi',* before the full stop'. Collectors were taken in by all this, and paid dearly for such curiosities. Cochin was another artist who produced endless 'states' to

GILLES DEMARTEAU. *Nude.* Engraved after Boucher

DEDIÉ A MONSIEUR BERGERET RECEVEUR GENERAL DES FINANCES.

Honoraire aßocié libre de l'academie Royale de Peinture et de Sculpture.

Demarteau l'ainé Sculpsit C.P.R.

Par son très humble et très Obéissant Serviteur, Demarteau l'ainé

N° 46

satisfy his regular customers. But this questionable procedure aroused unfavourable comments among other engravers. Gaucher, considering the purchasers even more to blame than the dealers, rightly condemned *'l'ineptie des curiolets'.* What had Greuze to say about this practice and the criticism it aroused? This strange, unattractive character, unstable and brutal, convinced of his own genius and spending his time 'listening to the stir being created around his name', must have been delighted with the prints which guaranteed his renown – particularly since he refused to exhibit in the Salon.

While on the subject of these good professional reproductive engravers, it may be recalled that some of them grew weary of their trade. Miger regretted having spent his 'whole life making holes in copper'; as for Basan, he announced that he had 'too lively a character for engraving'. He commissioned and signed prints, but he is not the author of the six volumes known as *l'œuvre de Basan.* He became a dealer (in about 1776 he had the biggest business in Paris), and trained amateurs and organized sales.

Collectors of drawings were very numerous. After Jabach, who died in 1695, and who had amassed five thousand drawings which he had begun to have engraved (283 were thus reproduced), the most important was Pierre Crozat (1665-1740). He was a banker from Toulouse, and although very wealthy, he is usually known as Crozat *le pauvre,* because he had a brother, Antoine, who was even richer. He began collecting drawings in the early years of the eighteenth century. Installing himself in a handsome town house in the rue de Richelieu, he displayed the portfolios of drawings which he bought in Italy, or in Antwerp, in a gallery which linked the two wings of the building. To save time, he used to buy whole collections, skimming the cream off them and keeping the best for himself. He devoted one day a week to his hobby; he spent that day in his gallery, looking at his drawings with his friends, being visited by connoisseurs whom he welcomed most affably, and conversing with the artists engaged on the classification of his thousands of drawings. Every collector of any importance at that time was a friend of Crozat, in particular, the dealer Huquier, Lempereur, goldsmith and collector, the Count of Caylus, the scholar Mariette, and rich foreign collectors like the Swede Tessin.

From the time of the *Régence,* collectors in the eighteenth century

JEAN HUBER. *The Philosophers at Supper*

increased in numbers, by 1750-60 they were legion, and all of them came to Paris to learn and to purchase. It was in Paris that Tessin formed his collection, now the admiration of visitors to the Museum at Stockholm. It was also in Paris that the Prince of Saxe-Teschen bought, in about 1750, the drawings which form the nucleus of the Albertina collection. A new and very interesting feature of these collectors is that they did not buy only drawings by old masters, like Crozat and his followers, they also bought a great many drawings by contemporary artists. Modern drawings accounted for nearly half their collections—sometimes even more than half—those by Lemoyne, Boucher, Fragonard and Watteau are particularly numerous.

JEAN HUBER. *Portrait of Voltaire*

JEAN HUBER. *Mademoiselle Clairon's Visit to Ferney*

Drawings began to change in character as a result of all this. They were made to be sold as works sufficient in themselves—not simply as sketches for paintings, but works of art with their own aesthetic value.

Charles de Tolnay believes that the practice of making a drawing for its own sake originated in Germany in the sixteenth century, in the Cranach circle; I am inclined to think that it made its appearance in Italy at about the same time, among the followers of Raphael. In any case, it was unusual in the sixteenth century, and even in the seventeenth.

JACQUES-FIRMIN BEAUVARLET. *The Chestnut-seller.*
Engraved after Greuze

In the eighteenth century, however, it was practised widely in France, and painters made drawings which were sold as such. Fragonard, and more particularly Boucher, are the chief representatives of this new tendency.

Piganiol de La Force (1765), like the other connoisseurs of the period, values 'the drawings of the great masters far more highly than their paintings, because these are rightly considered to be the first expression of their idea, of which only the pen or pencil can convey the original spark, nearly always extinguished by the slowness of the brush'. Dezallier d'Argenville, who had a collection of six thousand drawings, also said that 'the drawings of the great masters, being full of vitality, are most stimulating items for a collection', and he advised art-lovers to buy them.

It is drawings of this kind that the engravers reproduced for the benefit of art-lovers of more modest means—the French middle class. They chose the most attractive drawings to reproduce—above all, those of Boucher. But a drawing could not be reproduced satisfactorily by means of the usual engraving processes—the burin was quite insuitable, and it was difficult to do justice in an etching to any but a pen drawing. Drawings in two or three coloured chalks, like those of Watteau for example, could not be reproduced by means of etching; Jean de Jullienne had tried the experiment in his *Figures de différents caractères,* in which Watteau's drawing were only very imperfectly evoked. It was left to Demarteau to invent a new technique; Demarteau and Boucher created the art of engraved reproductions of drawings, Boucher providing the drawings and Demarteau reproducing them.

Boucher is above all a draughtsman—even more of a draughtsman than a painter; according to his own estimate, he left more than ten thousand drawings and hardly a thousand paintings. He produced designs for decorative schemes, for the theatre, and for tapestries. He had amazing facility, and worked with unbelievable speed—besides, he was in constant need of money, and such considerations encouraged him to concentrate on producing drawings. These were very popular, and sold readily, but in spite of the speed at which he turned them out, he could not keep pace with the demand, and he had engravings made from them. His favourite engraver was Gilles Demarteau, of Liège (1722-1776), who invented, or rather perfected, a method of reproducing them.

Demarteau belonged to a family of armourers. Engravers were often

GEORGES-FRÉDÉRIC SCHMIDT. *Louis de La Tour d'Auvergne, Comte d'Evreux.* 1739

to be found amongst these families—the craftsmen who did the chasing on the armour were often engravers, or served their apprenticeship thus. Demarteau came to Paris in about 1739 to join one of his brothers who was working there as a goldsmith. He enjoyed the protection of the Belgian Embassy in Paris—in other words, of M. de Heusy, the Paris envoy of the Prince-Bishop of Liège. He was a reproductive engraver,

BERNARD LÉPICIÉ. *The Busy Mother.* 1744. Engraved after Chardin

GILLES DEMARTEAU. *Head of a Woman.*
Engraved after Boucher

and, like other engravers, worked for the trade. He realized that there was no future in portrait engraving; the fashion for genre engravings was at its height. He did studies of women, and dedicated his engravings to *fermiers généraux,* financiers, the Chief of Police, M. de Sartine, the collector Blondel d'Azaincourt. For us, such dedications are a guide to the taste of the collector thus honoured, for the engraver, they brought in about a hundred *livres* from the person to whom they were addressed and ensured the sale of a certain number of prints.

Demarteau worked with the roulette. Instead of engraving his lines with the burin, or etching them, which would have given them the character of a pen line, he used the roulette, a little wheel with very fine teeth which produced the effect of a drawing done on grainy paper. The lines can be inked in different ways, with excellent results.

Demarteau was not the inventor of his process. It was used in England (where it was known as the 'crayon manner'), from 1735 onwards, by Bord and Knapton. In 1739 Arthur Pond engraved a print which is well known both in France and England—*Doctor Misaubin,* after a drawing by Watteau—this is the portrait of a charlatan (or so he was considered) who treated everybody by homoeopathy, prescribing them pills. In 1740, Jean-Charles François was engraving in the 'crayon manner'; this engraver from Nancy tried out the process in order to provide cheap models to copy for art school students. In the same year (1740) he published *Principes de dessin faciles et dans le goût de crayon,* an album of six sheets, printed in black, of somewhat clumsy workmanship, but took counterproofs of these which were softer and an improvement on the first printing. In 1749 he came to Paris, where he published further sheets of studies, printed in a somewhat disagreeable orange-bistre. However, he was congratulated by the Academy, produced 311 plates, and died in 1769. His work is weak in quality, and there was little demand for it.

With Demarteau, it is quite another story. He was very skilful, and his training as a chaser of metal gave him qualities which his predecessors lacked. He engraved in the 'crayon manner' from 1757 onwards; his plates were printed in a rather ugly shade of brick red. He worked with François, but he felt himself to be the better artist, and the public also recognized this (see *Mercure de France,* August 1775); Delafosse preceded François in 1757, and was associated before him with the engineer Magny. In an engraved inscription, he records that Saint-Non 'was particularly interested' in his discovery. However, in July 1757 Demarteau obtained a *privilège,* and in the Archives there is a document (D1 1221, fol. 716) granting a pension to Demarteau 'in consideration of the part he played in inventing crayon manner engraving, and making it more widely known.' When François died, Demarteau bought up all

La Confrérie des Compagnons Charons.
Printed by Charbonnier, rue Saint-Jacques

his plates, and published them with the inscription *'Demarteau perfecit'*. He became an associate of the Academy in 1767, and Academician in 1769; the invention was held to originate with him: 'A splendid and useful invention—these are true crayon drawings' (Diderot, 1767). Demarteau and François had separated after some obscure disagreement (Bonnet *taught* him François' secret), and in October 1759 he produced an excellent print: a farmyard after Boucher, dedicated to Blondel d'Azaincourt. Then, in less than twenty years, he engraved a thousand plates—more than fifty a year, or three or four a month. He is the ideal engraver of Boucher's drawings, rendering them with all their charm.

He also engraved after Huet and other artists, and in addition he engraved for the Académie Royale. In 1771, he suggested making engravings of the drawings to be used for the instruction of the students, desiring to 'increase the most fitting means of helping in the training of the students'. In 1757, François had received permission to make engravings of the King's drawings.

Demarteau's success can be measured by the vast number of his students—and imitators. Between 1765 and 1789, everyone in Paris was doing engravings in the 'crayon manner'—French artists such as Jeaurat and foreigners like Schmidt. The Dutch collector Ploos van Amstel (1726-1798) published engravings of this kind from 1760 onwards. We shall return to the subject in connection with English prints and stipple engraving, which is a variation of the crayon manner.

Louis-Marin Bonnet developed the process still further, and engraved in the 'pastel manner'. He boasted of his 'secret' in 1769, but had begun using this method in 1767, after trying to perfect the process for several years. Bonnet was born in Paris in 1736 (and died at Saint-Mandé in 1793), studied under François (1757) and then under Demarteau, and began by inventing a method of printing to give the effect of a drawing *à deux crayons,* on blue or grey paper (in about 1767). His process for imitating pastel drawings 'complete with all the colours, both light and dark, completely deceives the eye, and equals the originals for the freshness and liveliness of the tints'. These are skilful facsimiles, which do indeed deceive the eye, especially when they are framed. Bonnet made reproductions after Boucher, and later Huet, but his most successful piece is undoubtedly the famous *Head of Flora* achieved by a combination of different techniques and eight separate printings.

At this time, and even earlier, prints were trying to compete with painting, not merely by representing colours in varying tones, using black and white only, but by attempting to reproduce them in actual colour. The English had been trying to do the same thing with mezzotint since 1660. Their most successful years—between 1700 and 1750—date from the arrival in England of two remarkable Irishmen, Brooks and MacArdell (their English competitors were Valentine Green, 1739-1813, and J. R. Smith, 1752-1812). The mezzotints after Reynolds are very fine, and although no longer in fashion, were much admired in their own day.

The English also experimented with chiaroscuro woodcuts in colour; from 1722, Elisha Kirkhall reproduced Italian paintings in a mixture of etching, mezzotint and woodcut. Walpole was very critical of these not uninteresting attempts, which he described as 'laborious and tedious'. Jackson (1700-*c.*1770) imitated painting after working in Venice in 1731, but he confined himself to wallpaper, which he began to manufacture in 1754. Jacob Christoph Le Blon (1667-1741) is more interesting; he was a German from Frankfurt working in Holland, who learned about colour perspective through reading the works of Newton. He engraved about fifty plates, working in England and in France.

From 1720-1735, Le Blon engraved and published colour prints in London, having obtained a licence from the king to do so. The public was delighted with these forty-three plates reproducing works of the masters and anatomical figures. In 1721 a collector comments that these prints are preferable to copies painted in oil, because they are more faithful renderings and are less expensive. In about 1735, aged sixty-two, Le Blon came to Paris, where he obtained a royal licence (possibly not without difficulty), trained some assistants who were to become his pupils, and finally announced with triumph a portrait of Louis XV (1739). This work, still famous to-day, has generally been believed to have been painted and engraved by Le Blon, and therefore an incunabulum of original engraving in colour, but Mr G. Wildenstein has shown that the portrait was engraved after the English artist Blackey. Le Blon did very little engraving in Paris; he was more successful in England, where his assistants, trained in the mezzotint process, helped

GILLES DEMARTEAU. *Nude.* Engraved after Boucher

JOHN BAPTIST JACKSON. *The Meal*

him more efficiently. He died in 1741, made bankrupt by his own invention, although Louis XV had supported him and given him a pension.

Le Blon engraved, as Mr G. Wildenstein's inventory has shown, on four different plates which were passed through the press in turn. The process was later adopted by Gautier Dagoty, who tried to prove that he invented it, since Le Blon sometimes used a simpler method during his experiments, colouring an engraved plate and printing from it.

After Le Blon's death, his plates and his method, which his pupils Blackey and Tardieu would have liked to take over, were used at first surreptitiously and then officially by Gautier Dagoty, who, in an experiment carried out before the King in 1767, boasted that he employed neither burin nor brush, and that he printed four plates one after the other: 'Five turns of the press, six minutes, and the picture emerges complete.'

Aquatint (also called *'gravure au lavis'* in France, because it imitated the effect of a wash drawing) is very probably French in origin. François-Philippe Charpentier, 'mechanic', and the Swedish engraver Floding, announced in the *Avant-Coureur* of July 19, 1762, that they were the inventors of 'the new manner of engraving in exact imitation of a wash drawing'. In 1765 the same periodical affirms that their prints after Boucher and Fragonard are indistinguishable from the original drawings. In 1768 Leprince also claimed credit for this invention; P. P. Burdett employed the same method in England, in 1771, and in 1774 Sandby was using it in his landscapes, having discovered the 'secret' of Leprince and Burdett. It was exploited in England by the dealer W. Austin (1722-1820), and then by Rudolph Ackermann, a German publisher born in 1790, who employed an army of colourists and issued editions of three thousand copies (Gray). Dacier gives the year of origin not as 1762, but as 1765, which is when Floding defended the process against fraudulent imitations.

There existed also the 'popular print', or, more correctly, provincial engraving, but it was practised only to a limited extent in those French cities which were centres for the production of devotional images. The significance and value of those which do originate in the provinces has been exaggerated because of the activities of private collectors and museums, who have eagerly sought out even the least important

JACOB-CHRISTOPH LE BLON. *Portrait of Louis XV*
Engraved after Blackey

examples of them, in order to safeguard scraps of information of historic interest. These engravings were definitely not executed by the people and for the people. Woodcuts and also line engravings which tend to be disregarded because they are not 'popular', were produced in the big provincial towns, usually by engravers of playing-cards who were accustomed to the use of wood, or by descendants of Parisian artisans. Their interest was entirely local; the *imagiers* worked for a sanctuary or for the trade confraternities, but never in connection with an illustrated book, or the execution of a portrait. No attempt was made at originality —the subject was awkwardly treated in imitation of Paris originals which were themselves second-rate. In spite of such shortcomings, however, these prints have a certain appeal—those of Sevestre at Orléans, of Hoyau at Chartres, of the Arnavons at Avignon, of Sainte-Agathe at Besançon, and of Joubert at Lyon. But it should not be forgotten that the *Stages of Life* by Guillaume Allabre (Chartres) are based on an intaglio print from the rue Saint-Jacques, published by Crépy, and that Gaugain at Le Mans (d. 1772) used to get prints from Mondhare (also of the rue Saint-Jacques) which he not only sold, but also used as a source of inspiration. Only one of these provincial workshops is of any real importance—that of Letourmy at Orléans, which was active from about 1770 to 1800. Letourmy, as far as we know (he has not yet been the subject of a historical study), came from the Cotentin, like the publishers of the rue Saint-Jacques in Paris. He had a hundred agents, one of them in Paris, and his prints were extremely successful, because they were not all concerned only with religious or local matters, but also touched on every subject of current interest.

If, then, the so-called 'popular print' (as M. and Mme Seguin readily inform us) does not originate in the provinces, where can one find the prototypes? We believe the answer to be in Paris, in the rue Saint-Jacques. From the time of Henri IV, this had been the domain of booksellers and dealers in prints. Mariette's house (now Number 37) is always given as an example, but there were ten or twenty others in the same street—Trouvain, *Au Gril,* Rochefort, *Au Palmier,* Nolin, *A la Place des Victoires,* Leblond, *A la Cloche d'Argent,* Neveu, *A l'Occasion,* Vanneck, successor to the widow Landry, *A Saint-François de Sales,* Pierre, Torchebœuf, Pasquier, Larmessin, and so on—one could find there pictures engraved in a rough and ready fashion with the etching-needle or the burin, hand coloured and sometimes even gilded. They depicted the saints of the calendar, scenes from the Bible, subjects to instruct or amuse, all executed in a simple style, and intended for the lower classes. Mercier *(Tableau de Paris)* deplores their success, and the wide currency they enjoyed; he pokes fun at 'the foolish picture-collectors', and laments over the armies of draughtsmen, engravers, intaglio printers, illuminators, booksellers, pedlars and picture-makers' who assail him on all sides 'each with his picture in his hand'.

JEAN-BAPTISTE LEPRINCE. *Russian Concert. c.* 1770

There is one form of these popular prints from the rue Saint-Jacques which has only recently been the subject of a historical study: the 'optical views', engraved and published under the auspices of Chéreau, Daumont, the Bassets, Mondhare, and other less important dealers. They depict events, scenery, and above all views of towns which, when looked at through a special apparatus, appeared to stand out in relief, something like the stereoscopic views of the nineteenth century. They were extremely fashionable in smart society, and eighteenth-century artists often represented *L'Optique*—people or children looking at views through the apparatus. These views were a manifestation of the fascination exercised by distant lands and theatrical fantasies during the century of the *Encyclopédie*—they helped to develop a feeling for the exotic.

GERMANY AND ENGLAND
CHODOWIECKI: THE ENGRAVERS AFTER REYNOLDS

In order to keep them separate from their French contemporaries, with whom they have no connection, we are here grouping together some artists who have nothing in common except their reaction against the French spirit: the vignettist Chodowiecki—one might describe him as a kind of anti-Cochin—and the English mezzotint portrait engravers who could be called the anti-Drevets.

The rapid development of the illustrated book in Germany during the second half of the eighteenth century seems very remarkable, though as yet we know little about it, since it has not so far been properly studied. The number of authors increased twofold; so did the number of readers and bibliophiles. Frederick II never travelled without carrying a whole library with him. More and more court libraries and public libraries were established; the Dresden library, which was opened to the public before the end of the century, inherited sixty-two thousand volumes from Count Brühl, one of the great bibliophiles of his time; that at Göttingen, considerably enriched in 1769, with the acquisition of the books of Johann Friedrich von Uffenbach and Zacharias Conrad, was endowed by Gottlieb Heyne, Brühl's former librarian, with a highly intelligent classification system and acquisition plan. Winckelmann, writing to Count Bünau, relates how well he was able to work in these sanctuaries of learning: *'Bibliothecam Regiam Berolinensem et Jenensem, quoties licuit, adii, Dresdensem etiam satis instructam inspexi.'* His contemporaries also mention the library of Nöthentz, 'estimated as worth nine hundred thousand francs, French money..., French papers have given an account of it in the past'.

It was in this very favourable climate, then, that Chodowiecki's fertile talent manifested itself. His output was enormous, amounting to three thousand items (all etchings) executed in two periods: the first lasted till about 1770, and during this time he produced prints of medium size, varied in subject and in a fairly conventional style. During his second period, after 1770, when he had become a fashionable illustrator, he made innumerable small prints for books and pocket almanacs.

Chodowiecki himself (b. Danzig 1726, d. Berlin, 1801) seems to have thought more highly of his paintings than his engravings—he painted about thirty pictures which are little appreciated to-day, but, being a rather dull portrait artist, it was his engraving which first attracted the attention of the Berlin Academy in 1756. His little print, *The Game of Dice* earned him a commission to illustrate an almanac for the Academy. From then on he engraved ceaselessly, in Dresden and Berlin, sometimes assisted by his son Wilhelm, who was also a draughtsman and an engraver.

During his first period, he produced his *Passe-dix* (1756), his first attempt at etching. This showed Nicolas Foinvelle, a poor degraded wretch of a Frenchman famous in Berlin as a habitué of smoking dens. He also engraved portraits—one of Frederick II on horseback, for example, one of Frederica Sophia, and one of Wilhelmina (1767) showing her face framed in roses and orange blossom. In addition, he did an important genre subject, *Calas' Last Farewell* (1768), a large plate which he engraved after his own painting, at the earnest request of all those who had seen and admired the latter, and wanted a reminder of it. The story of the wretched Calas was certainly a moving one. Jean Calas, a protestant merchant of Toulouse, was accused of having murdered one of his sons who had become a convert to Catholicism: he was condemned at Toulouse to be tortured on the wheel, and was executed in 1762. This sentence shocked France, and indeed the whole of Europe. Voltaire organised a celebrated campaign, which succeeded in bringing about a revision of the trial, and restored Calas' good name.

He had not murdered his son; the latter had committed suicide (he had hanged himself). While a print by Delafosse, after Carmontelle, published in Paris in 1765, was sold for the benefit of the unfortunate Calas family (shown in prison on the print), Chodowiecki painted a picture in 1767 in the manner of Greuze, showing Jean Calas about to leave his children for the place of execution. This picture was so successful that Chodowiecki reproduced it himself in dry-point the following year. Antal has demonstrated Chodowiecki's debt to Hogarth, and also to the philosopher Lavater who greatly admired this picture. He recalls that Hogarth's *Analysis of Beauty* had been translated into German in

DANIEL-NICOLAS CHODOWIECKI. *Galitzine at the Battle of Choczin*

1754 (a year after its publication), that it was very much read in Germany, and that in 1757 Hogarth had been elected a member of the Academy of Augsburg.

Other examples worthy of mention from this first period, are the engraving of a historical subject, *Battle near Choczin, September 18, 1769,* another showing one of the favourite walks of the Berliners, *The Zelten, or Tent Site in the Park* (1771), and in particular the *Painter's*

DANIEL-NICOLAS CHODOWIECKI. *The Emotional Responses of the Four Temperaments. c.* 1767

DANIEL-NICOLAS CHODOWIECKI. *Calas' Last Farewell. c.* 1767

Studio, which shows Chodowiecki drawing at home, in the company of his wife and children. This family group has a most appealing simplicity and intimacy; these qualities recall the print of the young girl sewing beside her sleeping sister (1758). His illustrations appear in two forms, according to their purpose. For books, the ordinary vignette, very similar to the contemporary French vignette, is used as a frontispiece (*Grammaire française,* by Laveaux, 1784; Buffon's *Natural History,* by Blumenbach, 1787; or for illustrations in the body of the book (Nicolaï's *Life and Teachings of Sebaldus Northander;* Erman and Reclam's *History of the French Refugees in Prussia,* and Richardson's *Clarissa Harlowe,* etc.).

For almanacs, the tiny vignette was adapted to the format of the calendar. It is in these series of twelve very small prints for almanacs that Chodowiecki's real importance and originality is revealed. As in France, these almanacs were all the rage in Prussia, and Chocowiecki's talents were in great demand. Between 1770 and 1794-1796 he engraved the greater part of his vignettes, some of the best being for the almanacs of Berlin, Gotha, Göttingen and Lauenburg.

Their themes are extremely varied. Many are derived from German literature—in particular Gellert's *Fables,* Gessner's *Idylls,* Lessing's poetry, and Schiller's *Kabale und Liebe.* But the literature of other countries also provided him with inspiration—Italy, with Ariosto's *Orlando Furioso,* Spain with *Don Quixote,* France with the works of Voltaire, Lesage, Rousseau and Beaumarchais, and above all England, with Shakespeare, Sterne and Goldsmith. Several almanacs are devoted to early history; for example the *Almanach de Gotha* 1782, showing twelve scenes from the history of the Crusades, or another containing subjects from medieval history, Gotha, 1794; others depict more recent events, such as the twelve anecdotes from the life of Peter the Great, 1790.

Chodowiecki did not neglect fashion plate engraving *(Vestments of the Berlin Priests,* 1774), but he liked to point a moral (see the twelve moral subjects for the almanac of Lauenburg, 1779), and Goethe congratulates him for contrasting good and evil. He excels in imaginary themes where he can give free rein to his humour and fantasy. For example in the *History of Blaise Gaulart,* which can be read rather like a page of Topffer (Berlin, 1778), in the *Twelve Customs, Natural and Affected, in Instruction, Conversation, Prayer, in Walking, Showing Respect, and at The Ball,* in the *Twelve Proposals for Marriage* (from the village swain to the abductor), the *Six Motives for Marrying* (inclination, ambition, boredom, motives of profit, persuasion, spite) and their effects *(Almanach de Berlin* 1789), in *Ladies' Occupations* and *Men's Hobbies* (from tulip-growing to print-collecting).

The themes of these almanacs are of entertaining diversity; they are expressed with refinement, spontaneity and charm. By adopting the very small format, Chodowiecki discovered his own particular qualities, the lively, delicate grace of his drawing. He is quick to seize a pose, a gesture, a telling movement. His etchings, like his drawings, are executed with fluency, and free of all affectation. His minute vignettes retain the elegance of the French vignettes which he knew and admired, but avoid

JEAN-BAPTISTE DELAFOSSE. *The Unfortunate Calas Family.* 1765.
Engraved after Carmontelle

their frivolity. Chodowiecki's pictures portray no naked figures; they do not depict nude nymphs, voluptuous goddesses or dimpled cupids. They are never licentious but, on the contrary, often contain a moral lesson. Intimate in character, they are permeated with a characteristically German sentimentality, to which Chodowiecki adds a very personal touch of humour (for example, *Pilgrimage to Buchholz,* or *Naturalness and Affectation...).* Like the English and French vignettes, they are of genuine documentary interest, but of a more bourgeois and democratic nature. They are alone in their concern for psychology: whereas the French vignettists, even the skilful Moreau le Jeune, engraved faces without any expression, Chodowiecki tried to make his physiognomies convincingly alive. This preoccupation is the outcome of a personal psychological sense, probably coupled with the influence of Lavater. In fact, Chodowiecki drew the plates for the *Studies in Physiognomy* (he even engraved fifteen of them) and he occasionally tried to apply its principles to the characters he was depicting. He did so in the engraving *The Emotional Responses of the Four Temperaments,* in which he examines the reactions of four men at the sight of his painting *Calas' Last Farewell.* The first, a squat, heavy figure sitting in a chair with his hands on his knees and his head poked forward, stares at the canvas with a fixed and stupid expression; the second, thin and stooping, has a strained and anxious face; the third, his emotions stirred, wipes his eyes; the fourth, his indignation aroused, does not look at the picture, but holds out his clenched fist with an angry look.

In view of the very small size of his pictures, Chodowiecki is often unable to do more than suggest in very scanty fashion the sentiments of the characters he represents, which helps to give his vignettes a note of sincerity—a feeling often lacking in the French vignettes of the period.

Chodowiecki may be only a minor master, but he is the sole representative of the art of the vignette in Germany in the eighteenth century. His engravings never overwhelm the books and almanacs they adorn.

During the second half of the eighteenth century, seven hundred mezzotint engravings were produced in England after paintings by Sir Joshua Reynolds (1723-1792). This type of engraving, very much appreciated in England, was mainly employed in this vast undertaking, and in a few others apparently directed by the energetic publisher Boydell. Four hundred plates were produced by Valentine Green (1739-1813) and 150 plates by J. R. Smith (1752-1813) whose work was the better in quality; Samuel William Reynolds (1773-1835), a pupil of Smith, went to Paris, and formed a link with the romantic mezzotint engravers. The process was not popular in France in the eighteenth century—Cochin accused it of being too soft—a quality which others found charming. The French engraver F. X. Vispré, who wanted to work in mezzotint was obliged through lack of customers to leave France in 1775 and practise his craft in England.

CANTIQUE SPIRITUEL,

SUR DIFFERENS AIRS.

DIEU invite le pécheur à se convertir, & le pécheur se rend aussi-tôt à ses invitations

REVIENS, pécheur, c'est ton Dieu qui t'appelle, Viens au plutôt te ranger sous sa loi; Tu n'as été déjà que trop rebelle, Reviens à lui, puisqu'il revient à toi.

Le pécheur converti.

Voici, Seigneur, cette brebis errante, Que vous daignez chercher depuis long-temps, Touché, confus d'une si longue attente sans plus tarder je viens & je me rends.

DIEU.

Pour t'attirer, ma voix se fait entendre; Sans me lasser, partout je te poursuis: d'un Dieu d'un Roi, du pere le plus tendre j'ai les attraits ingrat, & tu me fuis.

LE PECHEUR.

Errant, perdu, je cherchois un asile, Je m'efforçois de vivre sans effroi: Hélas! grand Dieu, pourrai-je être tranquille, Si loin de vous, & vous si loin de moi?

DIEU.

Attraits, remords, terreur, secret langage, Qu'ai-je oublié dans mon amour constant? Ai-je pour toi dû faire davantage? Ai-je pour toi dû même en faire autant.

LE PECHEUR.

Je me repens de ma faute passée; Contre le ciel contre vous j'ai péché; Mais oubliez ma conduite insensée, Et ne voyez en moi qu'un cœur touché.

DIEU.

Puisque tu te repens, fais ce que je t'ordonne, Et crains les jugemens du Dieu qui te pardonne.

FIN.

ORAISON A JESUS-CHRIST.

O très adorable Agneau de Dieu donnez-moi votre paix en ce monde, le repos de mes passions intérieures & la grace en l'autre. AINSI SOIT-IL.

A ORLEANS, chez LETOURMY, Fabriquant de Dominoterie, place du Martroi.

Cantique Spirituel. c. 1780
Engraved in the Letourmy workshop, Orleans

Chodowiecki and the engravers after Reynolds, therefore, form a kind of island of resistance in a world where the French style reigned supreme. It was to enjoy another twenty years of supremacy, and reached its most perfect form under Louis XVI.

THE YEARS 1770-1789
THE PARIS SCHOOL OF ENGRAVERS: LAVREINCE, MOREAU LE JEUNE, DEBUCOURT

The years from 1770 to 1789 were years of the *joie de vivre* of which Sieyès later wrote so nostalgically – years of pleasure and perfection in pleasure, of the *game of love* found in Casanova as well as in Laclos, which consists, like a bull-fight, of 'a dramatic *action* with fixed *moves* leading to the *moment of truth* and the *kill*' (R. Vaillard, *Laclos,* ed. du Seuil, 1953).

But this love-game did not suit everybody; it was reserved for a section of the nobility, the *roués,* and a section of the bourgeoisie-*fermiers généraux,* merchants, members of the legal profession, other categories of society preferred sentimental subjects. These were the same people who had formerly expressed their ardour through the Church and its practices, which they had now abandoned. In fact, Mercier remarks with reference to Grace before meals, in the time of Louis XVI (*Tableau de Paris,* XII, p. 194), that 'it has not been in use for a long time, except in convents; elsewhere, it is completely forgotten'. One may also cite the case of the Abbé Campion de Tersan, a scholar and an amateur engraver himself, who 'refrained from exercising the sacred ministry *par délicatesse*'. Sensibility appealed to persons of this kind, particularly the women of the middle classes, and a large proportion of the working class. For them, and for all who had read *La Nouvelle Héloïse* (1760), the sight of *la vertu,* as they called it, the *tears* it brought to their eyes and its *ennobling* effect, were all food for the imagination, and added spice to life.

It is important to know of the existence of these two types of public in order to understand the two different directions in which the print developed; the engravings which 'graced the most elegant boudoirs and the portfolios of the *curieux*' were either *galante* or *vertueuse,* and the fact that they both existed at the same time has puzzled historians, who have tended to minimise one to the advantage of the other.

Girl with a Muff. Mezzotint after Romney

The engravers who reproduced the works of Lavreince represent one of these two aspects; the engravers after Moreau le Jeune represent the other. A man like Debucourt, on the eve of the Revolution, worked for both publics. There were very few original engravers – that is to say, engravers who executed prints from their own designs – they reproduced, or rather interpreted the compositions of minor painters.

The best of these was the Swede Nicolas Lafrensen (1737-1807), known as Lavreince in France, where he lived from 1774 to 1791. Nothing is known of his life or his personal convictions, but it has been established that, like all foreign engravers in Paris, he began as a commercial engraver – in his case, in Baudouin's entourage. Baudouin, Boucher's son-in-law, died in 1769, but between 1771 and 1778 engravings were made of his scenes of polished and aristocratic erotism. To meet the demands of dealers and public, Lafrensen continued the series, and although his works are heavier and more emphatic, often lacking the vitality of the age of Louis XV because of their over-precise character, they were enormously successful. Between 1778 and 1790, twenty-eight engravers produced reproductions of them. At the time of the Salon of 1785, a critic expressed regret that these engravers had not brought 'to their art that spirit of disinterestedness which accords so well with talent'; in other words, they went straight for what was most saleable. The titles of these prints clearly indicate their subject-matter: *Ah, let me see, Ah, what Sweet Delight, Oh, the Pretty Little Dog, Poor Pussy, why aren't I in your Place? The Darling Canary, The Mysterious Swing, The Dangerous Novel,* etc. Lavreince passes from flirtatious scenes such as *The Happy Moment* or *The Love-Letter* (about 1778, engraved by De Launay), to more wanton subjects engraved in colour by Janinet in about 1786: *The Comparison, The Difficult Vow, The Indiscretion, Seductive Proposals.*

One may or may not like these prints (and our ancestors were not unanimously in favour of them); certainly their frivolity, and their occasional silliness and equivocal nature, are open to criticism, but one has to admit their technical skill and charm. They harmonised so perfectly with the furnishings of the Louis XVI period that they can be counted a success, and form a landmark in the history of engraving.

However, they did not constitute the whole of French engraving at that period. Other engravers, or sometimes even the same engravers, show us with much felicity touching episodes, gallant rescuers, kind husbands, charming children, moving family scenes, and virtuous lovers. Thanks to engraving we are made aware of the more noble features of that society—we see the Duke of Orleans saving his jockey, a young woman bringing the unconscious well-diggers out of a cess-pool, or the girl Salmon proved innocent of having poisoned her master. Above all, a print made known far and wide the courageous conduct of the cavalry sergeant Louis Gillet. He had retired at the age of seventy, and was going on foot to the Invalides when, passing through a forest, he came upon a young girl tied to a tree, about to be tortured by two

JEAN-MICHEL MOREAU LE JEUNE. *The Magic Lantern Show.*
Engraved by Martini

NICOLAS LAVREINCE. *The Love-Letter.* Engraved by De Launay

NICOLAS LAVREINCE. *The Happy Moment.* Engraved by De Launay miscreants; he frightened them away and saved her. The action of the *virtuous* sergeant (whom Sade's *Justine,* his contemporary, would have been very happy to meet), made public by means of the print, was portrayed on dishes and cups, and was even to be seen in the Salon of 1785, glorified in a painting by Wille *fils.*

Simonet, also, engraved another touching subject after Moreau le Jeune (1783): the Duke of Angoulême chaining Time to a pedestal bearing a bust of his mother, the Countess of Artois, which was presented to the Count of Artois 'on the feast of her patron saint, and in honour of her convalescence'. (When it was no longer topical, it received a change of title, and became, under Napoleon, a representation of *The Wish of the Two Nations*—the French and the Austrians, delighted with the Emperor's marriage to the Archduchess Marie-Louise. Later, with slight changes, an edition was printed in honour of Voltaire).

French engraving has provided us with a *Life of Confucius* in pictures (by Duclos, after drawings from the Bertin collection, 1786), and a *Collection d'estampes représentant les événements de la guerre pour la liberté de l'Amérique septentrionale* (published in Paris in 1783; engraved by Ponce).

It was hoped in France that the accession of Louis XVI would bring back a period of prosperity and happiness. As early as 1769, Boizot depicted the Dauphin ploughing (a copy appeared in 1770); in October 1773 Marie-Antoinette, while she was still the 'dauphine', tended the injuries of a peasant wounded by a stag, and a print made known to the world how this victim of feudal rights was saved by the young princess (*The Dauphine as an Example of Compassion,* engraving of 1773). In 1776, Louise Massard engraved a characteristic subject: *Henri IV exhorting the New King;* a number of prints proclaimed: *Your King Vows to make you Happy;* appreciation of the king's humanity and benevolence was expressed in 1780, 1786, and 1787 (by Guyot). It was the same with the queen; *the interest and protection* (more or less genuine) *accorded to literature and the arts by Her Majesty Marie-Antoinette* is the subject of an engraving by Taraval after a drawing by the son of the Councillor Davy de Chevigné who commissioned it. In 1777, Duclos engraved a large print which showed the queen announcing to Mme de Bellegarde that her husband had been set free (Bellegarde had been sentenced for selling old rifles from the French arsenals to the American

NICOLAS DE LAUNAY. *The Indiscreet Wife.* Engraved after Baudouin

The Cavalry Sergeant Gillet. Engraved by Voysard after Borel 'rebels'; he was a deputy in 1789, and voted for the death of the king).

In 1789 Vangelisti engraved a *Monument to the Glory of Louis XVI* (the plate, with very slight modifications, was reprinted in 1793 as *The Triumph of Liberty,* and in 1802 as *Bonaparte the Peacemaker).* Subjects in honour of the king or queen seemed to have a guaranteed sale, because the violence of the Revolution seemed at first to be directed against the great nobles and the clergy rather than against royalty.

There is only one great name in book illustration at this period—Moreau le Jeune. His books and his series of prints, with their perfection and elegance, are examples of all that is most unadulterated and most French in the art of the reign of Louis XVI.

Moreau le Jeune (1741-1814) had no artists among his ancestors. He was the son of a wig-maker in the rue de Buci, in Paris, but he founded a family of artists, and his daughter married into the Vernet family, well-known throughout the eighteenth and nineteenth centuries. He was the brother of Louis Moreau, the fine landscape artist whom we have already mentioned.

Moreau le Jeune was born in Paris in 1741. He was devoted to drawing from his childhood; 'for him, to have begun to live and to have begun to draw were one and the same thing.' It is difficult to see where he acquired this passion—a genuine passion which lasted his whole life, moreover, it was poorly requited at first, because he did not find it easy going, and he was not immediately successful. His work was clumsy, and he became known as 'the ox'. He tried his hand at painting, which is interesting and unusual, as neither Cochin, Eisen, nor possibly Gravelot, had done any painting. Moreau le Jeune saw with a painter's eye, and because of this he was to bring about a transformation in illustration; he made it less small in scale, less delicate in inspiration, but gave it greater monumentality. Across an interval of years, one can see the influence of Boucher's *Molière,* also the work of a painter.

Moreau le Jeune had little success in Paris. When he was seventeen he went to seek his fortune in Russia, in 1758, the year of the *Decameron* illustrated by Gravelot. He became apprenticed to the painter Robert le Lorrain, who had just been appointed Director of the Academy in Saint Petersburg. In Russia, he attracted sufficient attention to become, at the age of eighteen, teacher of drawing at the academy of painting and sculpture in the Russian capital. In 1760 his master died, and he returned

PHILIBERT-LOUIS DEBUCOURT. *The Ill-guarded Rose.* 1791

to France. There was no room for a painter there, where there were already hundreds of artists of talent, and some of genius. So he decided to give up painting for engraving, and in 1761 he went into Le Bas' studio, like everyone else. In 1765 he married the niece of Prault, the great bookseller; he was thus launched in the world of books, became widely known, and was given as many commissions for vignettes as he wanted.

He began, however, by engraving large plates in the style of Cochin, whom he was shortly to replace as draughtsman and engraver to the Cabinet du roi, and by executing prints of public events. In 1766 there was *Inspection of the King's Residence at the Trou-d'Enfer,* signed by Le Bas but drawn and engraved by Moreau. In 1766, he engraved *The Bride Retiring,* by Baudouin, who was delighted with it and got him to do *A Model of Honesty* as a companion piece. In 1774, he did a drawing of *Fêtes at Louis XVI's Coronation,* intending to engrave it, but the Direction des Beaux-Arts was short of money and the project came to nothing. In 1778, he drew *The Triumph of Voltaire at the Production of 'Irène'* (engraved by Gaucher, completed in 1783). His illustrations are very numerous (two thousand prints); two books, the *Chansons* of La Borde (1773) and the *Œuvres* of Rousseau (1774-83), are without equal. To begin with the first: Benjamin de La Borde, a rich banker and patron of the arts, and a friend of Louis XV and Mme du Barry, composed some songs; he had them illustrated, as Dorat had done, so that the pictures might save them. The scheme succeeded perfectly; the plates were etched by Moreau le Jeune himself, after his own drawings. Unfortunately, La Borde quarrelled with him after the publication of the first volume, and the other volumes were entrusted to second-rate artists. Then, in 1774-83 Moreau illustrated the works of Jean-Jacques Rousseau, and the interpretation and execution of these volumes is rightly celebrated.

In addition to these two enterprises, Moreau le Jeune was also responsible for the plates in the *Monument du costume.* The Strasbourg banker Jean-Henri Eberts, a print collector and a friend of the engraver Wille, as well as being an amateur engraver himself, wished to record the elegant French fashions of the day, and to make them known abroad by means of prints of greater subtlety and better quality than the ordinary run of fashion plates – prints which could even be hung on the walls in middle-class homes. He commissioned the Swiss artist Sigmund

Freundenberger to do a set of prints illustrating French dress and manners of the eighteenth century; the twelve plates after Freudeberg (as he was called in Paris) came out in 1775, and were fairly undistinguished. A second set, also of twelve, appeared in 1777, and were of very different quality, because these were after Moreau le Jeune, and depicted the life of an elegant woman. A third series, published in 1783, shows the life of a minor functionary. Then Moreau le Jeune left for Italy, whence he returned, according to his biographers, with 'the grand manner'; but as far as we are concerned, he was finished – his vignettes had lost their freshness and charm.

These qualities were still fully present, however, in the delightful *Monument du costume.* Unlike Freudeberg's series, this was not simply a set of costume plates treated in a life-like manner in order to make them a little less dull, but intended for the use of dressmakers and milliners. It depicted with inimitable liveliness the life of a lady and gentleman of fashion, showing them at the races, at the Opera, at an exquisitely prepared supper, in the Bois de Boulogne, and also at home amongst their family *(True Happiness, The Good Omen, The Delights of Maternity),* or on social visits *(The Nobleman at the House of his Farmer, The Queen's Lady-in-Waiting).* According to the preface, these engravings form 'the code of fashion and etiquette'; they were addressed to all sections of society – to *nouveaux riches* and bourgeois, to artists and actors whom they helped to avoid 'an infinite number of errors', and also to foreigners. They were enormously successful and another edition of them was printed in 1789 with a text by Restif de La Bretonne. Copies appeared in 1790; in 1793 they were produced with an English text, and until 1900 they were constantly imitated in countless *Journées d'une Parisienne.* The following passage from the introduction is worth quoting: the author apologises for showing only rich and elegant circles, and regrets 'having had to choose from among a class which must not be taken to represent the usual habits of the Nation. France... is full of virtuous people and respectable families..., but the monotony of a decent, peaceful household would have no interest for our readers.'

Two very well-known artists can be taken as typical of a host of minor engravers working along similar lines: the line-engraver Wille, and Debucourt, who also worked with the burin and in addition produced colour prints.

JEAN-MICHEL MOREAU LE JEUNE. *Last words of Jean-Jacques Rousseau.* Engraved by Gutenberg

Wille had no more talent than artists like Duclos and De Launay, and his lifeless engravings were of less value than their etchings, but he kept a *Journal* which is of much interest. It was published without a preface by Duplessis; the Goncourts, in particular, made considerable use of it.

Jean-Georges Wille (1715-1807) is a typical representative of the School of Paris at that period. He was a German, born at Königsberg, and lived for seventy years in Paris, less on the proceeds of his engraving

JEAN-MICHEL MOREAU LE JEUNE. *The Farewell.* Engraved by De Launay

JEAN-MICHEL MOREAU LE JEUNE. *The Gardens of Marly*

JEAN-MICHEL MOREAU LE JEUNE. *The Queen's Lady in Waiting.*
Engraved by P. A. Martini

than on a flourishing trade in prints and pictures with Dresden, Leipzig, the Duke and princes of Saxe-Teschen and the Prince of Saxe-Weimar. He entertained foreigners, taking them to the Academy and conducting them on visits to private collections – in short, he was a well-known and

JEAN-MICHEL MOREAU LE JEUNE. *Illuminations for the Marriage of Louis XVI*

highly respected character. A 'gentleman traveller from Munster' came to see him, 'proud of being able to boast in his own country that he had made his acquaintance' (1783). In his youth he was employed by an armourer on the decoration of arquebuses, which explains the hard quality of his line. This was criticised in his own day, and Raphael Morghen remarked: *'Les estampes de Wille, ce n'est pas de la gravure, c'est du fer'.* For a long time he worked for other engravers; his best work was done roughly between 1744 and 1755, and his portrait of the Count of Saint-Florentin, after Tocqué (1751), was one of the more notable plates. He had to give up portraiture because of deteriorating sight,

JEAN-MICHEL MOREAU LE JEUNE. *It's a Boy, Monsieur!*

PHILIBERT-LOUIS DEBUCOURT. *The Two Kisses.* 1786.

and turned to genre subjects; he was particularly good at reproducing the Dutch painters, and depicted women wearing the gleaming satins so much in favour at the end of the century, thanks to Fragonard and Boilly. Thenceforth, his main importance was as head of a studio as well-known and as important as that of Le Bas had been in the previous generation. He had students from Switzerland, Italy, Germany, Sweden and Russia—the whole of Europe came to take lessons from him. One of his students was his own son; another was Johan Gothard Müller, from Stuttgart, who was commissioned in 1785 to engrave the portrait of Louis XVI after Duplessis, for the Direction des Beaux-Arts (he worked on it for three years without a break, except during three days' illness, then the Revolution intervened, and he finished it in 1793, too late). Others who worked under him were Preissler of Nuremberg and his son; a Russian in 1770; the Austrians Weirotter and Schmuzer, the Englishman Byrne who came in 1769: 'very quiet-mannered, not knowing a word of French'; the Englishman J. R. Smith in 1787, who also did not speak French, 'but nevertheless', says Wille after receiving high praise from him, 'seemed very gentlemanly'; Ryland, another Englishman, who came in 1758, and in about 1765 the London publisher Boydell, who was brought to Wille by Basan. Among the Frenchmen who worked with him were two whom we shall have occasion to discuss again when dealing with the period of the Revolution: Tardieu and Bervic. In 1784 Avril engraved a very fine plate after his design and under his direction: *The Double Reward* showing a young man receiving at the same time the cross of Saint-Louis and a fiancée; and in 1788 he did the companion piece: *French Patriotism* (before a bust of Louis XVI, a father hands on a sword to his son).

His friend and colleague Georges Fr. Schmidt (1712-1775), a virtuoso like himself, left in 1744, leaving his pupil Ficquet in Paris. His students became teachers throughout Europe, and kept his style alive: Preissler taught at Copenhagen, Müller at the Royal Academy of Wurtemburg, Schmuzer was director of the Vienna Academy (1768), Porporati founded the Naples school of engraving (1796). In 1769 Wille had become a member of the Imperial Academy of engraving, engraver to their Imperial and Royal Majesties; in 1770 he was engraver to His Majesty the King of Denmark. This virtuoso of the burin was one of the founders of the nineteenth-century academic school.

Debucourt was a very different kind of artist. He was a painter of modest talent; the chief work he sent in to the Salon, *The Feigned Embrace* (1785), was severely criticised on account of its 'dirty colouring and its sketchy appearance' (the latter would not be held against it nowadays). From 1785 onwards, he made colour prints of his own paintings. One may ask whether he was an original engraver. There is no doubt that he was, because he painted primarily to have models from which to make his prints. Living at a time when Lavater's books were enjoying so much success, he was mainly concerned with rendering facial expression—to such an extent that he has been classed as a

The Triumphant Return of the Heroines: October, 1789

Suite de Versailles à Paris
Le Retour triomphant des Heroïnes Francaises de Versailles à Paris le 6 Octobre 1789.
Ramenent avec Eux ver le soire au chateau des thuileries la fle. Röÿale
dit le Gros boulanger

caricaturist; no one of his period was better able to contrast the sly look of a woman, the complacent air of an old man, and the affable expression of a young gallant *(The Two Kisses)* One cannot overstress the fact that Debucourt was the contemporary of Lavater, the Swiss philosopher (1741-1801) who, in order to reveal and to combat vice, set about studying man's moral nature as it is revealed in his countenance.

His *Physiognomy,* already mentioned in connection with Chodowiecki, appeared during the years 1775 to 1778, and went through numerous editions in German, French and English. Obviously, it was not his theories that interested artists; but they went through the heavy volumes avidly studying the pictures by means of which the author drew attention to *'les singularités et caprices du visage'*. In this 'expressionist' movement the Swiss artist Jean Huber (1721-1786) deserves to be mentioned; his *'airs de tête'* of Voltaire are justly famous. Debucourt's *Promenade du Palais-Royal* (1787), perhaps his best work, derives from the Lavater tradition, with its various characters artificially grouped as they stroll in the most elegant spot in Paris, their faces and expressions symbolising the bored and sophisticated, the rake, the roué, or the courtesan. Notice that the title of the print is given both in French and English, both to ensure its sale in London, in the country of Rowlandson and Gillray, and also to appeal to the anglomania then so fashionable in Paris.

The *Galerie du Palais-Royal* is at the same time a gallery of expressions and a gallery of fashion; it came out at the same time as the tenth and final year of the *Galerie des modes et costumes* of Esnauts and Rapilly, and the third year of Duhamel's *Cabinet des modes,* fashion journals which came out every month, then every fortnight, then every ten days. These were intended not only for France, for theatres and artists, but also for use abroad, as their title indicates.

Finally, we must not omit to mention, on account of their nineteenth-century descendants, the black-and-white landscape engravers who studied under Le Bas. The latter published Vernet's *Ports de France* (1761-1783), for which the preparatory etching was done by Cochin *fils* and Martini. The engravers worked over the etched design with the burin, which rendered the topography with greater precision than etching and was more to their public's taste. One of the famous teams

JEAN-FRANÇOIS JANINET. *Colonnade and Gardens of the Medici Palace.* Engraved after Hubert Robert of engravers was formed by Née and Masquelier, who specialised in landscape at that period, and who undertook all kinds of commissions, whether it was a question of publishing Saint-Non's *Voyage de Naples* (1781-86, 284 plates), La Borde's *Description de la France,* Choiseul-Gouffier's *Voyage de la Grèce,* or Cassas' *Voyage d'Istrée et de Dalmatie.*

Plate from the Nouveau Recueil d'Ostéologie et de Myologie.
Engraved by Gamelin

Louis-Joseph Masquelier (1741-1811) did the preparatory etching, and François-Denis Née (1735-1818), a vignettist, completed the work with the burin.

In the following generation – during the French Revolution therefore – engraving played a considerable part in the formation of the new ideals and in the attack on the *ancien régime,* the king and the émigrés; but so far no-one has pointed this out, and it is not generally known. Very few people have consulted the thirty-odd albums in the Cabinet des Estampes (coll. de l'Histoire de France, coll. de Vinck, coll. Hennin) containing the main body of these works (most of which are anonymous), assembled by amateurs and not given by the publishers, as was the case with prints of an earlier and later date. The Goncourts looked at some of them, but they were prejudiced, being in favour of Louis XV and his mistresses; they stated that there was nothing in them but 'insipid vaudeville satire..., a shabby, poverty-stricken kind of irony'.

One must therefore try to study these prints impartially; their interest can then, perhaps, be better appreciated. To begin with, one notices that the better-known engravers soon gave up working – there were not enough commissions, there was not enough money (an engraver might work on a plate for six weeks, only to have his cook spend a month and a half's earnings in ten days). Above all, they did not want to compromise themselves, because, to a far greater extent than is usually admitted, they were conservative in their views, and closely linked with the old order of society.

It is not that they would necessarily have been unsuccessful; it should not be forgotten that Debucourt's *The Ill-guarded Rose* came out in 1791, and his *Promenade du Palais-Royal* in 1792, and one could mention a great many other prints depicting fashionable society, in the Louis XVI style, which were published during those years. In fact, they were so numerous that Wicar, a pupil and an admirer of David, denounced them to the Convention. When a law of 19 July 1793 made it compulsory to deposit a copy of every print with the Bibliothèque Nationale, nothing but genre subjects were sent in throughout the Revolution, although the Director Bounieu and his assistant Duchesne (who joined the staff in 1793) were in favour of the new régime. But anonymous popular prints form the main part of the engraving of that period; these were etched in a vigorous style, without much attention to craftsmanship, and roughly coloured. Their anonymity is to be regretted, because they often

SERGENT MARCEAU. *The Happy Mother*

La Trouée de Grandpré

seem to be the work of accomplished draughtsmen who knew how to handle a scene, to give character to a face, or to pick out the most expressive detail. This is so in the case of most scenes depicting the great days in the history of the Revolution – the 14 July, and the return of the king to Paris in October, or, again, the departure of the conscripts. It is not simply that they are skilful – there is a kind of heroic air about them that gives them the power to move.

Apart from scenes such as these, the revolutionary print is particularly rich in caricatures. Sometimes earlier prints were used as models for these; Marie Antoinette as a harpy is a reproduction of an engraving of 1771 by Desprez, representing a chimera. The caricaturists also looked at English caricatures, and with these elements they formed a somewhat

Exercise of the Rights of Man. 1792

But at the First Sound of the Drum... Engraved by Guyard after Mallet

PAR BREVET D'INVENTION.

NOUVELLES CARTES DE LA RÉPUBLIQUE FRANÇAISE.

PLUS DE ROIS, DE DAMES, DE VALETS; LE GÉNIE, LA LIBERTÉ, L'ÉGALITÉ LES REMPLACENT:

LA LOI SEULE EST AU-DESSUS D'EUX.

Si les vrais amis de la philosophie et de l'humanité ont remarqués avec plaisir, parmi les types de l'Égalité, *le Sans-Culotte* et *le Nègre;* ils aimeront sur-tout à voir LA LOI, SEULE SOUVERAINE D'UN PEUPLE LIBRE, environner l'As de sa suprême puissance, d'ont les faisseaux sont l'image, et lui donner son nom.

On doit donc dire, Quatorze DE LOI, DE GÉNIE, DE LIBERTÉ ou D'ÉGALITÉ; au lieu de Quatorze d'As, de Rois, de Dames ou de Valets; et Dix-septième, Seizième, Quinte, Quatrième ou Tierce au GÉNIE, à LA LIBERTÉ ou à L'ÉGALITÉ; au lieu de les nommer au Roi, à la Dame ou au Valet: LA LOI donne seule la dénomination de MAJEURE.

Aux Jeux où les Valets de Treffle ou de Cœur ont une valeur particulière, comme au *Reversy* ou à *la Mouche*, il faut substituer L'ÉGALITÉ DE DEVOIRS ou celle DE DROITS.

CES CARTES sont *Fabriquées par U. JAUME et J. D. DUGOURC.* Le Dépôt général est rue Saint-Niçaise, N°. 11, A PARIS.
On y trouve tout ce qui concerne les Jeux; et l'on se chargera des Commissions pour les Départemens, relativement à ce genre.

New Playing-Cards

Two Methods of Approach

surprising and possibly not very original style. But these caricatures struck home. André Blum has given some telling examples of this; he has shown that on 31 July 1789 a 'censor of caricatures' was appointed (Robin, member of the Academy), and that on several occasions in 1791 the censorship forbade the sale of caricatures directed against the royal family. Toward the end of 1791, or at the beginning of 1792, the censorship changed hands and was thenceforth applied in the opposite direction, in spite of the protest of those who considered such prints

Revolutionary Committee under the Terror. c. 1795.
Engraved by Berthault after Fragonard *jeune*

a kind 'public rostrum for calumny'. The revolutionaries perceived that 'pictures and caricatures are the most powerful means of influencing the heart of man, because of the lasting impressions they leave'. The authorities encouraged anti-clerical caricature, which quickly became widespread, and condemned any which tended to 'mislead, belittle or insult the common people' – such as those which represented Louis XVI and Marie Antoinette as martyrs, or showed Marat, 'a martyr for the cause of Liberty, disfigured by the most horrible convulsions'. Not content with encouraging the production of caricatures, the Convention even commissioned them when the law relating to Suspects was proclaimed (12 September 1793) and Marie Antoinette was being tried. David was requested to produce large quantities of caricatures 'which would arouse public feeling, and make people aware how hateful and ridiculous are the enemies of the Revolution'. A first series of about ten prints was directed against the English; David drew two of them (their scatalogical nature surprises his historians) which were then

The Ninth Thermidor, or the English Surprise. 27 July 1794.
Engraved by Louvion

Frederick William III in Full Mourning. 1793.
Engraved in Delion's studio

Reception of the Decree of the 18th Floréal.
Engraved by A. Legrand after Debucourt

engraved; he received three thousand *livres* for each one, printed in an edition of 500 copies in black and white and 500 in colour. But the undertaking seems to have been badly organized, and nothing further was done.

Louis Capet and his family in the Temple. 1792. Prudhomme, *Révolutions*

Middle-class taste, even during this period of upheaval, remained very conformist, and the favourite painter was Mallet, who continued in the tradition of Lavreince; Guyard did an engraving after one of his pictures showing young men enrolling, and entitled *But at the First Sound of the Drum, he sacrifices for his Country his Well-being, Life and Loved Ones.* Other prints after Mallet were in praise of natural religion, or divorce – no doubt all these sold better than the caricatures, though the latter were more expressive. The power of caricature was fully recognized at that time, and the Catholic and Royalist Boyer de Nîmes wrote an essay on the subject in 1792, because 'in all revolutions, caricatures have been used to stir up the populace... they have prompt and terrible results'.

Goncourt preferred English caricatures to the French ones, because, he said 'caricature is the English art'. He was thinking of Rowlandson

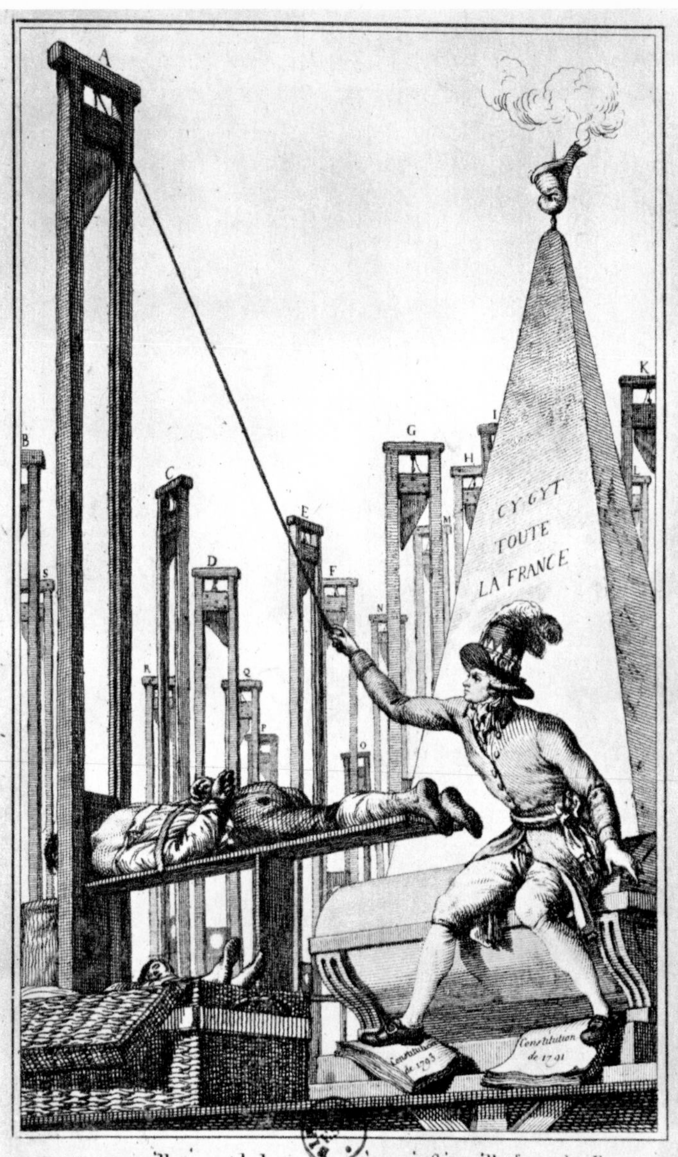

Robespierre guillotines the Executioner. 1794

Frenchwoman going to War. 1793. German engraving

and Gillray, contemporary with the French Revolution and certainly more gifted than the Parisians, whose work they influenced (they were very well-known in Paris). In 1785, the *Espion des peintres de l'Académie royale* announced that it was 'tired of the exaggerated praise bestowed on a mass of English prints exhibited in the Palais-Royal shops'. Debucourt made no secret of imitating them, even on the technical side, and it was announced in the journals that his portrait of La Fayette was the first engraving 'executed in France in mezzotint, known as *manière anglaise.*'

The English, for their part, were also acquainted with French caricatures; and as early as February 1790 the London dealer Hollande advertised in his gallery 'the largest collection in Europe of political and humorous engravings, with those published in Paris in the French Revolution', as well as those of Rowlandson and Gillray.

Although the work of these two men was very different in conception and execution, they are always linked together because they were contemporaries and both humorous artists; this, however, is an over-simplification. Thomas Rowlandson (1756-1827) belonged to the middle classes; he was the son of a merchant, and a watercolour artist with a keen eye for the ridiculous in everyday life—in expression, in dress, in manners and customs—as well as for the grotesqueness of politicians and their ambitions. He likes to show his characters full face, with disfiguringly open mouth, or in profile with an exaggeratedly hooked nose; he contrasts the full-bellied rascals he is so fond of with good-looking, often guileless young men. He did aquatint engravings, colouring the first impressions of his prints himself in order to make them more like his watercolours. Basil Gray has shown that caricature only occupied an important place in his work from about 1786 to 1815; before that, he engraved reproductions of drawings, and afterwards he did the figures in series of prints of London.

James Gillray (1757-1815) was a very different kind of man; he was the son of an old soldier, a London grave-digger; he became insane at the age of fifty-eight, after devoting his whole life to caricature. He was a political caricaturist of considerable violence, whose best plates (out of a total of roughly 500) date from the years 1787-95. Like Hogarth, he is a satirist convinced of the ignominy of men, and particularly of men in high position, and wanted to lash out at them—whereas

THOMAS ROWLANDSON. *Transplanting of Teeth*

JAMES GILLRAY. *French Liberty. British Slavery*

Rowlandson saw the same things with the tolerant smile of the looker-on. James Laver has rightly said that Gillray was not, like Rowlandson, a painter who did engravings, but a draughtsman who etched; he is the heir of the French artists in the Saint-Aubin circle, but with a satirical power unknown before his time. We will always see the English royal family of that period as Gillray has shown it. When he abandoned internal politics and turned his attention to attacking France, his representations of Bonaparte are unforgettable. He is a closer observer than Rowlandson, and does not resort to the trick of showing the nose in profile, or to coarse humour; his intention is not to make us laugh, but his wit often lies in the composition of the scene; he knows how to emphasise the contrast between the lean French, emaciated by the hardships of the Revolution, and the obese English, attacking their dinner with gusto.

In addition to these two outstanding artists, Sayers and Dent, and more especially Isaac Cruikshank, also produced work which was sometimes of a very high quality. Mrs George has shown that these caricaturists did not work independently, or for a periodical, but apparently for a committee of men with right wing views called the 'Association for preserving Liberty and Property against Republicans and Levellers' (founded in November 1792).

With these English prints, and also with the French caricatures we have discussed, can be compared Goya's *Caprichos,* which derive from them.

JAMES GILLRAY. *The Gradual Abolition of the Slave Trade. c.* 1793

CRUICKSHANK, ISAAC (1756-1816). *John am I Draggl'd*

JAMES GILLRAY. *The Finishing Touch.* September 1791

JAMES GILLRAY. *The Zenith of French Glory*

THOMAS ROWLANDSON. *Fast Day*

LOUIS DAVID. *The Great Royal Knife-Grinding Establishment for sharpening English Swords*

JAMES GILLRAY. *Un petit Souper à la Parisienne,* or, *A Family of Sansculottes refreshing after the Fatigues of the Day*

La Grande Aiguiserie Royale de Poignards Anglais
Pitt

Petion
Vive la Liberté
Vive L'Egalité
Louis le Grand
Proprieté de la Nation
Un petit Souper, a la Parisienne. — or — A Family of Sans-Culotts refreshing, after the fatigues of the day.

FRANCISCO DE GOYA. *It is hot. Caprichos,* No. 13

In Spain, engraving begins with Goya's *Caprichos.* There had been other engravers before him, of course, from as early as the sixteenth century, whose *œuvre* has been devotedly assembled, at the cost of much patient research, by Señora Paez de Santiago; but there is very little individuality about these prints. In the reign of Charles III (1759-1788) an attempt had been made to encourage the development of engraving and book design by means of large state enterprises, inspired by Godoy (see *Mémoires,* II, 309). *The Royal Gallery of the Escorial* was published at the king's expense (sixty-four plates after the paintings, and twelve views of the palace, engraved by 'the best Spanish artists'), also the *Colleccion de las estampas grabadas a buril de los cuadros pertinencientes al rey de España* (forty-eight plates by R. Morghen, Volpato, Carmona and others), engraved 'to facilitate the study of the great models', and the *Horses* of Velasquez, the *Costumes* of Spain and the modern nations, a series on the kings of Spain, one on famous men, a *Bible* in pictures, and a *Don Quixote* which historians of the book now prize 'more for the typography and inking than for the engravings'. All this work, carried out under French influence by engravers trained in Paris, gave no grounds for expecting any sudden new development in Spanish engraving. Choffard remarked that Salvador Carmona (1744-1807) came to France, and learnt the art of the burin under Nicolas Dupuis with three other Spaniards, but that in Spain 'his talent was not confirmed'.

Then Goya made his appearance. Suddenly, after a serious illness in 1792, after which he convalesced in Cadiz in the home of his friend Martinez, a collector of prints, he took up engraving—both in order to express himself as an artist, and also to help convey the thoughts of a group of very close friends whose ideas he shared. As André Malraux has so well put it, this court painter abandoned the official part of his art for several years: 'He discovered his genius the day he dared to give up pleasing others.' He broke abruptly with the past: 'His solitude—he had become deaf—interrupts the dialogue of his whole epoch.'

One can attempt to define him as representing a tendency—that of intellectual and liberal Spain. Let us find out who his friends were at that time—the privileged sitters he allowed to pose for him. Moratin,

FRANCISCO DE GOYA. *They say Yes... Caprichos*, No. 2

FRANCISCO DE GOYA. *Good Advice. Caprichos,* No. 15

his closest companion, poet and man of letters, who provided him with ideas and captions, was in Paris in 1792; he was present at the capture of the Tuileries, and spent days and nights in the Palais-Royal, a centre of pleasure, of news, and of cafés; he visited Pinel, the celebrated doctor for the insane. Another friend and model, Lhorente, wrote a discourse on the Holy Office in 1793, proposing the reform of the Inquisition, still so powerful in Spain (in 1783 a 'witch' was burnt, between 1794

FRANCISCO DE GOYA. *It is pulled well up. Caprichos,* No. 17

yala Percivo

FRANCISCO DE GOYA. *Even looking thus, he cannot yet see. Caprichos,* No. 7

FRANCISCO DE GOYA. *This Dust! Caprichos*, No. 23

FRANCISCO DE GOYA. *San Francisco de Paula*

and 1797 there were fourteen public enforced penances, another twenty between 1798 and 1800, without counting numerous secret punishments); his discourse was too outspoken, and could not be printed. Melendez Valdès, another sitter, was a fashionable poet, 'a spoilt child of the muses and of society'; he wrote an ode on fanaticism, and was denounced to the Inquisition in 1796 as having read forbidden books and repeated the ideas contained in them. Iriarte, another of Goya's models, was prosecuted for being in favour of the French *Encyclopaedists;*

FRANCISCO DE GOYA. *Poor little things! Caprichos,* No. 22

he had to perform a secret penance before the Inquisition. Juan de Escoquiz, Canon of Saragossa, translated Young's *Night Thoughts* into Spanish (the book was published by the royal press in 1798). Almost everything was centred around the *Tertullia* (literary salon) of Jovellanos, again one of Goya's models, and his protector; it was he who brought into prominence Lhorente's treatise, in 1798, and tried in vain to have it published; to him was dedicated the *Ode on Fanaticism* by Melendez

FRANCISCO DE GOYA. *How they pluck her. Caprichos,* No. 21

Valdès (who claimed to be his protégé, his 'creation'). He had, incidentally, long been a protector of the liberals; he had been an important minister under Charles III, then under Charles IV, was dismissed by the Inquisition and exiled to the mountains of the Asturias in 1794, but then restored to office in 1798 against his own wishes, by special order of the king. He only remained in favour for eight months, after which he was again exiled, this time to Majorca. He was a statesman, poet,

Ducreux distressed.
Engraved by himself

theorist, and the friend of many foreigners, English and French; he translated Rousseau into Spanish.

Jovellanos was not the only one to hold advanced ideas. Urquijo, who replaced Godoy on 28th March 1789, was a follower of Voltaire, a well-known atheist, and a 'jacobin' appointed to office by the previous group; he was 'sent on leave' in 1800, arrested by order of the Inquisition in 1801, and imprisoned for seven years without books, without ink, and without light. Godoy, whose conscience was troubling him for not having been to confession for eight years, submitted to the king a plan for abolishing slavery, and another for abolishing the Inquisition, in 1796. Fernan Nuñuz, another of Goya's sitters at that time, ambassador to France in 1787-88, sent books and periodicals from Paris; his correspondence reveals that there was considerable smuggling carried on, and that the works of Mirabeau, for example, entered Spain in this way, in loose pages, hidden in the hatboxes of fashionable ladies.

All these men were very much influenced by a member of the previous generation: Olavides, Governor of Andalusia and Seville, who in 1770 believed that an infusion of French ideas was necessary to arouse Spain from her torpor. He went to Paris, where he frequently visited Voltaire and Rousseau, collected an enormous library, translated the French poets into Spanish verse, and bought the finest furniture he could find for his house in Madrid. He ordered fabrics from Lyon, and engaged French workmen. But he too was kept in confinement as a heretic by the Inquisition; he spent eight years in a monastery, only being permitted to read approved books, and having to go to confession every month. He escaped and went to France, where he was hailed as a martyr in the cause of tolerance; but he was converted, wrote a large book, *Apology for Religion,* and in 1798 returned to Spain, where he died in about 1803.

Finally, the Duchess of Alba, whom Goya liked and admired so much, had been brought up in the new ideas by her father, who corresponded with Rousseau and thought very highly of him. She resembled the heroes of romance, or those of Dostoievsky; she was ready to protect an inarticulate, ignorant monk as readily as a *torero.* She dressed in the French style, and in men's clothes, she loved philosophy as her husband loved music, she adored buffoons, and everything that brought her into closer contact with life.

This advanced and courageous intellectual circle, many of whose members died in exile in France or as victims of the Spanish revolution in about 1810, was not only concerned with the world of ideas and of politics; it was also interested in the new theories as related to other problems. Several of them, including Moratin, belonged to a strange Madrid society called the *Acalophiles,* or lovers of ugliness. These cultivated men and elegant women were obsessed by the idea of ugliness, and by the interest it had for them. Like Debucourt, Gillray and Rowlandson, they knew and studied the large volumes of Lavater's *Physiognomy.* Seen in its context, this movement is easily accounted for; it is contemporary with the publication of the English caricatures, which it must have known, and also the new publications illustrating Leonardo da Vinci's grotesque heads (London, 1786). Not much earlier, in France, a Dijon magistrate used to walk about the streets grimacing 'in order to look like the caricatures in his collection'; and Ducreux exhibited his studies of heads with various expressions, just as Messerschmidt, in Germany, had (in 1770) executed sixty-nine character heads in lead.

Goya's art therefore had its antecedents, and also its parallels among his contemporaries, as Lafuente Ferrari has shown; but without his genius all these movements would have remained in obscurity. This genius was revealed in the *Caprichos,* a set of ninety-two plates in etching and aquatint, published in 1799. This admirable series has a disconcerting effect when one goes through it page by page; 'the pack of cards has been shuffled', in the words of Lafuente, who believes that Goya did this deliberately in order to create a more powerful impact with 'the brutal character of the transitions'. He may also have been acting out of prudence, to conceal the existence of 'explosive' cycles. There are, in fact, three or four types of subject: first, woman, the worthlessness of her love and her contempt for man; man and woman are each as bad as the other *(Tal para qual),* and their love is contemptible as that of the dogs in the foreground of one of Goya's prints. In another group, Goya shows the impossibility of communication; man is isolated in a tower, a prison, and does not even know himself *(Nadie se conoce).* Next comes the virulent and very topical social satires, directed against ignorance, against charlatans, the conceited, those who turn a deaf ear, whether their deafness is deliberate or involuntary, the ambitious, the clergy who take advantage of superstition *(Tragala, perro),* the sufferings of the common people, and universal suffering to which the only answer is sleep and silence. Finally, Goya introduces us to the world of magic and witchcraft. Here, his attitude is strange; he makes a point of showing us his dreams, his visions, advancing 'the firm evidence of truth', and, at the same time, he assures us that it is 'the sleep of reason which produces nightmares', a somewhat surprising profession of faith.

But the value of the *Caprichos* does not lie only in the ideas they express; these are presented by one of the greatest of all masters of the art of the print. Goya, who had not previously used aquatint, and whose etchings had hitherto been directed to producing an entirely different effect, here engraves with a power which has never been equalled. This is not aquatint as Demarteau or François used it; the etching is not that of Fragonard or Tiepolo (though it derives from them); the two techniques are here used to create an entirely new medium of expression. Aquatint is perhaps the medium which best suits Goya; very occasionally, he uses it alone, in contrasting masses, without line and without regard for 'finish', and these are the finest plates of the series. Most of the *Caprichos* are combined etching and aquatint, or etching alone; it is as if he had 'thought out' the series in aquatint, and finished it off with the etching-needle (earlier writers mention collaboration, which is not impossible).

Looking at these plates, one is reminded of Lavater; one also recalls the collection of 'several thousand prints' (including the works of Piranesi) owned by his friend Martinez, with whom he stayed in Cadiz in 1792 (see P. Gassier in *Les Journées de Bordeaux,* 1957). His rendering of expression is admirable; suffering, joy, silence, vanity is revealed in the whole body, but most of all in the face—the gaping mouths of the monks, the broad, vacant faces of the beauties, the unforgettable old women with their sunken jaws and huge noses, sometimes resembling the animal heads he gives to some of his characters. When he shows us a man hiding himself to eat, in order not to let us see his hideous face *(El vergonzoso),* he reaches even greater heights of horror and pity. Malraux has described him as *'le plus grand metteur en scène de l'absurde';* he passes judgment not only on the society portrayed by Debucourt or Rowlandson, but on the whole of mankind.

The *Caprichos* were certainly known to the Acalophiles, who approved of them and even annotated them, as Lafuente tells us. In fact, it is probably the Acalophiles who wrote the longer captions (not those consisting of a simple interjection, which are certainly by Goya himself); and they provided the explanations or 'keys' to the series, which some had believed to be simply an attack on the Spanish sovereigns and the royal favourite. The plates were published on about 20 February 1799, and were only on sale for two days. As Lafuente has shown, the Saavedra ministry fell on the 21st, and whether or not the publication was linked in Goya's mind with a campaign against Godoy being carried on at the time, and inspired by France, it was forbidden by the new government, and its creator was afraid of running foul of the Inquisition. To protect himself, he suggested on 7 July that practically the entire edition should be acquired by the king – it was not accepted till 1803.

The *Caprichos* were little known and little understood by contemporaries, or at least by the French. De Bourgoing, author of a well-known *Voyage en Espagne,* wrote: 'Don Franciso Goya has above all a talent for depicting with fidelity and charm the manners, costumes and pastimes of his country'. While Spain continued to derive inspiration from the memory of the *Caprichos* (Mlle Armingeat has shown how they influenced an aquatint of 1808 – a propaganda print directed against Murat), France, following Denon's example and then guided by Delacroix's eloquence, did not 'discover' the *Caprichos* until shortly before 1830, at the same time as England.

THE END OF THE CENTURY

In Spain after 1794, we have just seen a genius at work in the person of Goya; in England, the exceptionally gifted caricaturists Gillray and Rowlandson; elsewhere, talented virtuosi 'well-liked by the public'. In what direction was the print to develop? Would it survive the dramatic consequences of the Revolution, which – in France, at least – resulted in the disappearance of a social class, and so effectively ruined the chances of artists that in 1800 an engraver wrote beneath one of his prints 'Dedicated to myself' (which speaks worlds on the absence of all patronage)?

In actual fact, engraving came back into public favour, and even conquered new and distant territory. America, where mezzotint was well-known, aquatint only slightly and woodcut hardly at all, now had it own school of engraving, and no longer had to rely on English or Dutch artists.

That versatile character Paul Revere (1735-1818) can claim to be one of the earliest American-born engravers; though he was primarily a silversmith, his print of *The Boston Massacre* has become a part of American history. Cornelius Tiebout, of a German Huguenot family, was also American-born; he studied in London, where he went after 1789, and practised engraving when he returned to New York in 1794. He had rivals in the persons of the Irishmen Houston and Edwin David. The United States could also boast of an engraving by a painter: Joseph Wright's *Portrait of Washington.* Moreover, new forms of engraving made their appearance; for example the *physionotrace*, invented in France in 1786 by Gilles-Louis Chrétien, though it only came into use at the end of 1787, thanks to the portraitist Quenedey. This ingenious

CORNELIUS TIEBOUT. *West Point*

JOSEPH WRIGHT. *Portrait of Washington*

State of the English Nation

apparatus made it possible to make a rapid drawing of the sitter, a kind of silhouette which the engraver Chrétien took back to his studio to finish. Quenedey soon quarrelled with Chrétien, who joined forces with an artist named Fouquet, then with another named Fournier. During the Revolution, a period of great uncertainty when friends could never be sure that they would meet again, the *physionotrace* was extremely popular as a means of preserving the likeness of 'dear ones'. Chrétien exhibited 100 in the 1793 Salon, and 600 in the Salon of the Year IV. This cheap and rapid form of portraiture reached America, where it was practised by Fevret de Saint-Mesmin (1770-1852), a native of Dijon who had settled in the United States, where his work found considerable favour.

Ha! quel vent! C'est incroyable.
Engraving published by Bonvalet in Paris, *c.* 1796

Another process very much in use after 1794 was stipple engraving, made fashionable by the cosmopolitan Bartolozzi. In this, the modelling was achieved with dots, not lines (Laan aptly describes it as 'miniaturists' engraving'), and the resulting lack of definition was sometimes quite pleasing. It was first practised in Italy, and was rediscovered by the Englishman Ryland when, during the five years he spent in Paris, he saw and admited the 'crayon manner' engravings of his teacher, François. On his return to England, he produced numbers of stipple engravings after Angelica Kauffmann from 1768 onwards (these were printed in Paris), until he was charged with issuing counterfeit coin, and hanged in 1783. The great master of stipple engravings, however, was the Italian Bartolozzi, working after G. B. Cipriani, during the long years he spent in England after 1764, and particularly from about 1780-1800. His 700 reproductive prints were enormously popular; they were imitated by his fifty pupils, by the pupils of the French engravers who had fled to London during the Revolution, by engravers of genre subjects in about 1795, and by Regnault and Prud'hon.

George Stubbs (1724-1806) also used stipple for the work he was engaged on when he died *(A Comparative Anatomical Exposition...)*; but the magnificent *Anatomy of the Horse* (1766) reveals him as one of the finest of all line engravers. He was entirely self-taught, both as a draughtsman and as an engraver; but 'it is doubtful whether any contemporary engraver could have equalled these plates, could have

Public Audience of the Directory. Engraved after Chataignier

FEVRET DE SAINT-MESMIN. *Portrait of Levington*

GILLES-LOUIS CHRÉTIEN. *Portrait of Le Pelletier de Saint-Fargeau.* 1792

FRANCESCO BARTOLOZZI. *Venus recommending Hymen to Cupid*

recorded with such sensitive precision the different textures of bone, muscle, tendon or artery, and at the same time preserved the majestic, living order of the whole animal...' (Basil Taylor, 'The Graphic Work of George Stubbs', *Image,* 3, 1949-50). This fine work, written, drawn and engraved by the artist, is a monument of scientific illustration, in the direct line of descent from the *Vesalius* of 1545.

The same period saw a revival of the use of the wood block in England, thanks to Thomas Bewick (1753-1828), whose book on *Quadrupeds* was published in Newcastle in 1790. The two volumes of his *British Birds* (1797-1804) each represent seven years of study.

PIERRE-PAUL PRUD'HON. *The Bath*. Engraved by Roger

PIERRE-PAUL PRUD'HON. *Phrosyne and Melidore*

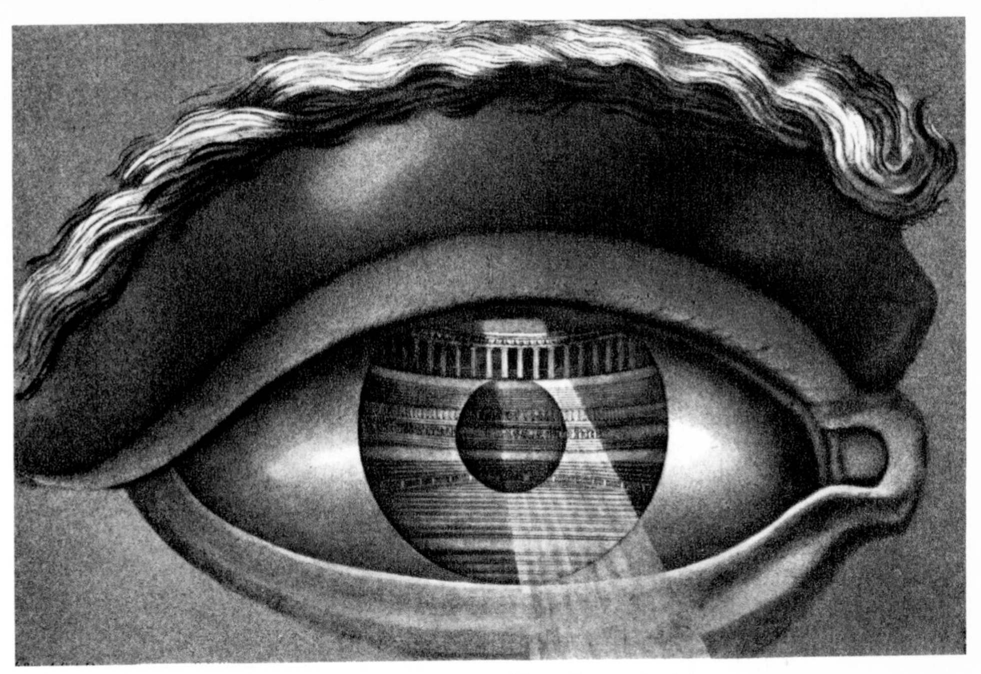

CLAUDE-NICOLAS LEDOUX. Plate from *Architecture*

New processes were evolved to suit a new type of public, and new masters of the art made their appearance, one of whom was William Blake. This great visionary (1757-1827) had fallen under the spell of the Middle Ages; he had learned to draw by copying the tombs in Westminster Abbey. He introduced a new development in the art of the book, by engraving the text (composed by himself) as well as the illustrations he had designed *(Songs of Innocence,* 1789*)*. Text and images are interwoven in a strange kind of harmony, forming a perfect accompaniment for each other. The unusual nature of the work is accentuated by the use of colour; Blake himself coloured the pages, of which only a few copies were printed. This method (engraving text and plates at one and the same time) had been 'revealed' to him in a dream by his dead brother.

In France, engraving reappeared after the Revolution in the form of the illustrated book—illustrated by painters, but painters very different

THOMAS BEWICK. *Leopard,* from *Quadrupeds*

from Blake. The reappearance of the book is due to the great printer Pierre Didot, known as Didot *l'Aîné* (1769-1853), who succeeded his father, François, a printer of classics in 1789. He published a quarto edition of Molière in 1792, and about ten more volumes between 1794 and 1800. Instead of applying to Moreau le Jeune, Monnet, Marillier, Queverdo or other vignette artists, he commissioned painters to do his illustrations: Regnault for La Fontaine's *Adonis* (1794) and Montesquieu's *Le Temple de Cnide* (1796); the young Gérard, then aged twenty-seven, for La Fontaine's *Psyché* (1797); Prud'hon, a man in his forties, for Gentil-Bernard's *Art d'aimer,* published in the same year (the drawings were exhibited in the 1796 Salon); Gérard and Girodet

BRITISH BIRDS. 53

THE SEA EAGLE.

(*Falco Ossifragus*, Lin.—*L'Orfraie*, Buff.)

THOMAS BEWICK. *Sea Eagle*, from *British Birds*

WILLIAM BLAKE. *Songs of Innocence.* 1789

for the Virgil of 1799. In 1793 he began work on an edition of Racine which was not published till 1801. This book nearly proved too much for him, because he was at grips with 'six or eight painters, and twelve to fifteen engravers'; he asked Prud'hon and David to take charge of the undertaking. Prud'hon was heartily disliked by the creator of the *Sabines,* who considered him thoroughly out-of-date and an interloper, and after doing the frontispiece he withdrew. David was left in sole

WILLIAM BLAKE. *Songs of Innocence.* 1789

command, with his pupils; he directed the execution of the work, but refused to accept payment or to put his name to it, preferring to assist the progress of Gérard, Girodet and Moitte.

Didot *l'Aîné* set the fashion; his brother Firmin (1764-1836) decided in 1799 to approach the painter Peyron for illustrations 'engraved under his direction' for the plays of Crébillon; one edition of *Les Liaisons Dangereuses* contains illustrations after Mlle Gérard (engravings dated

1795), and in 1798 the printer Honnet commissioned Prud'hon to do the illustrations for a novel by Lucien Bonaparte.

The art of engraving had thus developed in many different directions; and out of these conflicting elements was created the nineteenth-century print.

VARIOUS OPINIONS OF THE PRINTS OF THE EIGHTEENTH CENTURY, FROM THEIR OWN DAY UNTIL NOW

Let us examine the writings of the period to discover how this art of engraving was regarded, how was it defined, why prints were bought, what purpose they were believed to serve, and what books were published about them in the various countries between 1700 and 1800. Finally, we will give a brief account of the interest aroused by eighteenth-century prints from year 1800 until our own day.

'Of prints', says Richardson, in his *Essay on Criticism*, 'there are two kinds: such as are done by the masters themselves, whose invention the work is, and such as are done by men not pretending to invent, but only to copy (in their way) other men's works...

'The former sort may again be subdivided into three kinds. First, those they have done after a painting of their own. Second, those done after a drawing also done by themselves. Finally, those designed upon the plate which has been sometimes done especially in etching... if it be designed on the plate it is a kind of drawing (as the others are) though in a manner different from the rest, but it is purely, and properly original...

'The excellence of a print, as of a drawing, consists not particularly in the handling; this is but one, and even one of the least considerable parts of it: it is the invention, the grace, and greatness, and those principal things that in the first place are to be regarded.'

Richardson therefore distinguishes between original engraving and reproductive engraving; he also distinguishes between technique and style, regarding the latter as more important.

Let us now see for whom the prints we have just defined were intended. In the first place, for the *curieux*—that is to say, amateurs and print collectors; and the Chevalier de Jaucourt, who collaborated actively on the *Encyclopédie* of Diderot and d'Alembert (according to Voltaire, he 'did three-quarters of it') will explain why: 'A discriminating amateur has a collection (of prints) in his study; he goes through them with a secret pleasure unknown to men without discernment, sometimes admiring the boldness and power with which the great masters have handled their burin, sometimes enjoying the discovery of the original work beneath a subsequent correction; then, satisfied with the charms of line engraving, he turns to those of etching, which, less elaborate in style, paints nature in its attractive simplicity... Certainly, in some of these prints he regrets the absence of effects of chiaroscuro which so delight the eye, but these he finds in the work of other masters particularly distinguished for this quality, who have produced as if by magic the effects of light and shade on objects.' *(Encyclopédie,* article 'Graveurs').

Such *curieux* were very numerous in the eighteenth century, and two particularly distinguished ones can be chosen to represent the kind of men they were: Mariette and Paignon-Dijonval. P. J. Mariette was the most important dealer in prints and drawings of his day, and at the same time a scholar, which gained him honorary membership of the Academy. His collection was so enormous that the sale of it lasted a whole year; his knowledge of prints was renowned, and Diderot (Salon of 1765) said that he could recognize 'each individual burin and every style' (1775-1776).

Paignon-Dijonval was a magistrate, who was also passionately interested in prints and drawings; his collection was so well classified that the catalogue of his sale (1810) is at the same time a catalogue of all the most important engravers of the eighteenth century.

However, the *curieux* were not the only ones to appreciate and make use of the print. It was also used to adorn the walls of those who could not afford to buy paintings, or the ante-rooms and offices of officials, who hung up a portrait of their protector; it was used also to grace the study of a man of letters, who displayed portraits of other famous men. In addition, painters used prints to provide them with subjects, and they were a source of themes, motifs and figures for designers of ornaments.

The print was also of considerable educational importance; visual aids were used as they are to-day. There was an easy and amusing method of teaching called *le quadrille des enfants:* 'By means of the twenty-four figures of which this method is composed, a child four to five years old can read fluently from all kinds of books at the end of three to four months, and even sooner.' The method was taught from 1748 in Paris, in the Berthaud boarding-school in the Faubourg Saint-Honoré; in about 1780 the Duke of Chartres, Philippe Egalité, used it for his children (Thiéry, *Guide de Paris, I,* 79). Amongst ordinary people, similar methods were used, though perhaps less subtly. Guérard, a stationer in Paris in the Rue du Petit-Pont ('opposite a pork-butcher's shop') who sold playing-cards, children's games and puzzles, claimed to be the only one who sold 'historical charts on various subjects, to refresh the memory on what one has read'. Similar developments took place in other countries; in England Mrs Trimmer announced, in 1792, a 'Series of prints of English history designed as ornaments for those apartments in which children receive the first rudiments of their education'. This series succeeded others illustrating the Scriptures, which came out in 1786 and were re-published in 1828.

Engravers were therefore supported both by the general public and by private collectors; but official bodies were often hostile to them. Louis XV and Louis XVI did not have recourse to engravers as Louis XIV had done, except in connection with the albums illustrating their coronation, and plates depicting funeral ceremonies.

The Académie Royale in Paris was not very friendly to engravers; it usually had about a dozen engraver members, of whom some were foreigners. It explained on several occasions, notably in September 1790, that engraving had never produced a masterpiece, and that there was no point in sending an student engraver to Italy. Vincent's well-known remark sums up the general opinion: 'If engravers have to be admitted to the Institute, then locksmiths will have to be admitted as well.' The Royal Academy in London, founded in 1768, did not admit engravers to full membership, though the English school of engraving was well known and produced work of a high standard. In other countries, engraving aroused more interest with the authorities. The Spanish Royal Academy, for example, founded in 1751, included an engraving section, and Godoy commissioned several series of reproductive prints.

However, even if they despised engravers, the various countries took an interest in the export and import of prints, because of their economic rôle and their propaganda value. In 1735, an English law was promulgated protecting engraving and preventing illicit copying; in 1765 an import duty was imposed, favourable to France who was able to export prints, but very disadvantageous for England. In 1754 a society was formed in London for the encouragement of the arts, industry and commerce (the Society of Arts, now the Royal Society of Arts); through its intervention the best engravers, who at that time were working in France, were recalled and established in England. After 1765 England even attracted French engravers as well; Delattré d'Abbeville, for example, came to practise stipple engraving.

Having discussed the attitude of the general public and official bodies, we now come to the question of historians and critics of engraving. It will be seen that, during the eighteenth century, histories of engraving, treatises on the subject, and books of technical information abounded in every country. A new edition of Abraham Bosse's *Traité,* for example, was published in 1701, 1745, and 1758 (with the help of Sébastien Leclerc, Cochin, and Jombert), and was translated into English and German. In 1795 Francis B. Spilsbury wrote *The Art of Etching* (London); Robert Donie's *Handmaid to the Arts* appeared in 1758, also in London (second edition 1764). In 1747 was published *Sculptura historico-technica,* with text taken from the best authors (again in London). Jackson, Le Blon and Gautier Dagoty published accounts of the processes they used; Papillon added a history of wood engraving.

Abraham von Humbert produced an *Concise History of the Origin and Development of Engraving* (Berlin, 1752), Thomas Martyn, *A Chronological series of Engravers* (Cambridge, 1770), a formula adopted by Fuseli *(Raisonnirendes Verzeichnis der Vornehmsten Kupferstecher und ihrer Werke, Zürich,* 1771), and by Huber and Rost, whose work derives from it *(Handbuch für Kunstliebhaber und Sammler,* Zürich, 1791-1804, nine in-octavo volumes). John Nichols published a catalogue of Hogarth's work (London, 1782), the print publisher Jombert a catalogue of the engravings of his friend Cochin *fils* (1770) and those of Sébastien Le Clerc (1774, two volumes); Helle and Glomy, friends of the great dealer Gersaint, published a catalogue of Rembrandt's etchings, which came out in Paris in 1751 and was translated into English by 1752. Horace Walpole prepared a catalogue of the English engravers; in France, Louis Doissin published a eulogy on engraving in verse, *Sculptura vive Sculptura, la Gravure, poème,* in 1753 (another edition in 1757); while, in England, Thomas Atkinson brought out *A Conference between a Painter and Engraver* (London, 1736).

The two most important general works are probably those by Heinecken and Gilpin. William Gilpin wrote an *Essay upon Prints,* with a study on the *manner* of the masters, and a manual for the amateur. This book first appeared in 1768, went through five English editions, and several foreign ones. Heinecken produced in 1771 his *Idée générale d'une collection d'estampes* (Vienna and Leipzig), written in French. Heinecken had prepared another manual for the amateur entitled *Dictionary of Artists after whose works Engravings have been made,* of which the first four volumes were published; this lists the prints under the names of the painters whose works they reproduce, and not under the engravers who executed them. Bartsch's *Peintre Graveur* was also published in French; it was begun in about 1779 and finally appeared in 1797, but did not include any eighteenth-century artists. These do appear, however, in the *Dictionnaire des graveurs* by P. F. Basan, the celebrated dealer, first published in 1767, and again in 1789 and 1809.

Let us briefly consider how eighteenth-century prints fared during the following century.

At the beginning of the nineteenth century, and until about 1850, the prints of the eighteenth century were either out of favour or unknown. Piranesi's plates, although they belonged to France, were given back to his son; they later passed through Didot's hands before reaching the pontifical collection. The *Caprichos* of Goya were not printed in any quantity till 1856; and Berti's *In Praise of Tiepolo* was published only in the same year. One collector alone, M. de Vèze, collected Fragonard's prints (his sale took place in 1855).

A revival of interest was to come, however. It has often been said that the Goncourts played an important part in restoring eighteenth-century art to favour—this is particularly true where the French print is concerned, and the fact was recognized in their own day. Taine visited their collection in 1863 *(Lettres à ma Mère,* p. 234), and saw 'some charming things; delightful Baudouins, Watteaus, Bouchers, Moreaus and so on. There is no better way of learning history; one feels as if one had just been living in that century. Refinement, gaiety, love of pleasure—all the rest springs from these three. Nothing can compare with the elegant attire, the albums full of lovely women, embroidered hangings draping their enormous beds, and the exquisite gilded furniture. It is an artful compound of all the elements of pleasure. This is the real

France'. In the Goncourts' study, opposite the fireplace, in the lower part of a large piece of furniture of blackened pearwood, there were in fact 'tightly packed together, the bulging portfolios containing the collection of prints of the last century... this collection of engravings contains great numbers of fine and rare eighteenth-century items, in coveted states, of incomparable freshness and with untouched margins... with the merest hint of warm, harmonious ivory, a kind of patina that time alone can bestow on the fine, tough, resonant paper of those days' *(Maison d'un artiste,* I, 96).

Admirers of the Goncourts soon followed suit. One of these was the art historian Philippe Burty (1830-1890), who was perhaps the original Barousse, the collector of eighteenth-century prints in the Goncourts' *Renée Mauperin.* We meet Barousse when he has just bought an *'épreuve découverte'* of *The Mysterious Swing* after Lavreince: 'This small gentleman wore a black coat and white side-whiskers; he carried a portfolio under his arm. 'Have you ever seen this?' he asked Denoisel... opening the portfolio a few inches. 'That? of course... it's the *The Mysterious Swing,* engraved after Lavreince.' The little gentleman smiled: 'Ah, yes—but look,' and he again opened his portfolio very slightly, but in such a way that Denoisel could insert only the end of his nose. 'Before *le flot.* Do you see—it is before *le flot!'* 'So it is.' 'And with full margins—what a brilliant impression, eh? I didn't get it for nothing, either, the robbers! I was pretty hard pushed, and by a woman, too...' 'Bah!' 'A hussy who insisted on seeing...' 'I wish I had known all that—I have seen a proof just like it—exactly the same—at Spindler's, the painter...' 'Bless my soul—are you absolutely sure? And before *le flot,* like mine?' 'Yes, before *le flot*; even before...' and the words Denoisel uttered in the old man's ear brought a blush of pleasure to the latter's face, and made his lips water.'

This particular type of eighteenth-century French print—*galante* in subject-matter, and of great charm—was to become very popular in France. In 1885, fifty eighteenth-century colour prints were published in facsimile with a preface by Chesneau (and a bonus of four 'free' prints). The Marquis de Priola was to make good use of his collection of illustrated eighteenth-century almanacs to lure fair friends towards his sofa. Others started the fashion for 'states', and a blind collector used to boast that if its code letters were read out to him, he could identify the 'state of any eighteenth-century prints'. But the fashion was to change; Colette, writing in 1912, informs us that in bachelor chambers, '*La Femme Nue* (engraved in the eighteenth century) is no longer in vogue... all that has been superseded by English prints—red coats on an acid-green background.'

Having examined the graphic art of this period, we are led to agree with Bouchot, Bourcard, Hind, Courboin, Focillon and L. Binyon, that there are two eighteenth centuries: that of the minor artists and that of the masters. Both, by their exploration and experiment into various methods and styles of the medium, made a valuable contribution to the development of this art.

Bibliography

ANTAL, F. *Hogarth and his place in European Art.* London, 1962

AUDIN, MARIUS. *Essai sur les graveurs de bois en France au XVIIIe siècle.* Paris, 1925

BAUD-BOVY, D. *Les maîtres de la gravure suisse.* Geneva, 1935

BLUM, A. *La caricature révolutionnaire.* Paris, 1916

BLUM, A. *Hogarth.* Paris, 1922

BLUM, A. *La Gravure française en couleurs au XVIIIe siècle.* Louvre. Coll. Edmond de Rothschild. Cat. of exhibition 1938-39. Paris, 1938

BOCHER, E. Les gravures françaises du XVIIIe siècle. Paris, 1875-1882, 6 vols

BRUAND, YVES. *La gravure originale en France au XVIIIe siècle.* Cat. of exhibition, Paris, B.N., 1960

CALABI, A. *La gravure italienne au XVIIIe siècle.* Paris, 1931

CHALLAMEL, A. *Histoire-musée de la République Française depuis l'Assemblée des notables jusqu'à l'Empire, avec les estampes, costumes, médailles, caricatures, portraits historiés et autographes les plus remarquables du temps.* Paris, 1842, 2 vols

COURBOIN, FRANÇOIS. *L'estampe française au XVIIIe siècle, graveurs et marchands.* Paris, 1914

COURBOIN, FRANÇOIS. *Histoire illustrée de la gravure en France.* Le Garrec, 1923-1929, vol. II

DACIER, E. *L'œuvre gravé de Gabriel de Saint-Aubin, notice historique et catalogue raisonné.* Paris, 1914

DACIER, E. *Gabriel de Saint-Aubin peintre, dessinateur et graveur.* Paris and Brussels, 1929 onwards, 2 vols

DOBSON, A. AND ARMSTRONG, W. *Hogarth,* London, 1902

DUPORTAL, JEANNE. *La gravure en France au XVIIIe siècle, la gravure de portraits et de paysages.* Paris, 1926

ENGELMANN, W. *Chodowiecki.* Leipzig, 1857. 2nd ed., 1906

FENAILLE, M. *L'œuvre gravé de Debucourt.* Paris, 1899

FERRAND, LOUIS, AND MAGNAC, EDMOND. *Guide bibliographique de l'imagerie populaire (avant-propos de Georges-Henri Rivière).* In Le Vieux Papier, 1957

FERRARI, ENRIQUE LAFUENTE, *The Graphic Work of Goya.* London, 1962
FERRARI, ENRIQUE LAFUENTE, *Grabados y dibujos de Tiepolo.* Cat. of exhibition in Madrid, 1935
FOCILLON, H. *Les eaux-fortes de Tiepolo.* In La Revue de l'art ancien et moderne, 1912
FOCILLON, H. *G. B. Piranesi. Essai de catalogue de son œuvre.* Paris, 1918
FOCILLON, H. *Les Maîtres de l'Estampe.* Paris, 1930
FOCILLON, H. *Technique et Sentiment.* Paris, Société de propagation des Livres d'Art, 1932

GEORGE, MARY DOROTHY. *Catalogue of prints and drawings in the British Museum. Political and personal satires.* London, British Museum, 1935
GILBERT, M. *Sergent-Marceau.* Catalogue in preparation
GILPIN, WILLIAM. An essay upon Prints. London, 1768
GONCOURT, E. AND J. DE. *L'Art du XVIIIe siècle, catalogue de Boucher.* Paris, 1880-1882, 2 vols., (cat. of Boucher, Debucourt, Gravelot, Moreau le jeune)
GROVE, FRANCIS. *Ruler for drawing caricatures, with an essay on comic painting.* 1788

HÉROLD, J. L. *M. Bonnet, catalogue de l'œuvre gravé.* Paris, 1935
HIND, A. M. *Watteau, Boucher and the French engravers and etchers of the earlier XVIIIth century.* London, 1911
HIND, A. M. *The etchings of G. B. Teipolo.* In The Print Collector's Quarterly, New York and London, April 1921
HIND, A. M. *G. B. Piranesi, a critical study with a list of his published works.* London, 1922
HUXLEY, A. *The complete etchings of Goya with a foreword.* London, 1943
HUXLEY, A. *'Prisons' with 'The carceri etchings by G. B. Piranesi', critical study by Jean Adhémar.* London, 1952
HYATT MAYOR, A. *G. B. Piranesi,* New York, 1952

JOMBERT, CH.-A. *Catalogue de l'œuvre de Cochin fils.* 1770
JUSSELIN, M. *Catalogue de l'Exposition Sergent-Marceau.* Chartres, 1946

KAINEN, JACOB. *John Baptist Jackson, 18th-century master of the color woodcut.* Washington, 1962
KEYSER, ED. DE. *Les Vues d'Optique.* In Le Vieux Papier, January 1962
KRAEMMERER, L. Chodowiecki. Bielefeld, 1897

LANCKORONSKA, M. AND OEHLER, R. *Die Buchillustration des XVIII Jahrh. in Deutschland, Oesterreich und der Schweiz.* Leipzig, 1932

LARAN, JEAN. *L'estampe.* Paris, 1959, 2 vols

LOPEZ-REY, J. *Goya's Caprichos. Beauty, reason and Caricature.* Princeton University Press, 1953, 2 vols

LUNDBERG, G. AND ADHÉMAR, J. *Lavreince, cat. of exhibition at the Bibliothèque Nationale, May - June 1949.* Paris, 1949

MALCOLM, JAMES PELLER. *An historical sketch of the art of caricaturing with graphic illustrations.* London, 1813

MALRAUX, A. *Saturne, Essai sur Goya.* Paris, 1950

OPPÉ, A. P. *Th. Rowlandson.* London, 1923

PAEZ DE SANTIAGO, ELENA. *Antologia del grabado español, quinientos años de su arte en España.* Cat. of exhibition in Madrid, October, 1952

PALLUCHINI, R. AND GUARNATI, G. F. *Les eaux-fortes de Canaletto.* Paris, 1946

PORTALIS, R. AND BERALDI, H. *Les graveurs du XVIIIe siècle.* Paris, 1880-1882, 3 vols

PROUTÉ, P. *Les eaux-fortes de Louis Moreau l'aîné.* Catalogue essay, Paris, 1956

PROUTÉ, P. *Les portraits d'après Cochin.* In cat. 1961

RENOUVIER, J. *Histoire de l'art pendant la Révolution considérée principalement dans les estampes.* Paris, 1863, 2 vols

RODRIGUEZ-MOÑINO, A. AND LORD EILEN, A. *Juan Antonio Salvador Carmona, grabador del siglo XVIII (1740-1805).* Cat., Madrid, 1954

ROUX, M. AND POGNON, E. *Inventaire du fonds français au XVIIIe siècle.* Paris, B.N., 10 vols, 1920-1958 (Cochin fils, Demarteau, Drevet, Eisen, Gautier-Dagoty, etc.)

ROY, C. *Francisco Goya. Caprices. Disparates... eaux-fortes precedées d'un à-propos (Commentaire des pl. par Jean Adhémar).* Paris, 1960

SALAMON. *Piranese.* Catalogue and preface of exhibition et the Museo Civico, Milan, 1961

SANTIFALLER, M. *Die Radierungen G. B. Tiepolo.* Vienna, 1938

SERVIERES, G. *Le peintre graveur Chodowiecki.* 1913, In La Gazette des Beaux-Arts, Paris, November, 1913

SINGER, H. W. *Le Blon.* In Mitteil. Gesellsch. f. vervielfältigende Kunst. 1901 (cat.)
SINGER, H. W. *Le Blon.* In Studio, London, 1903
SINGER, H. W. *Gautier-Dagoty.* In Monatshefte für Kunstwissenschaft, Leipzig, 1917

VALLERY-RADOT, J. *Œuvres gravées de Rowlandson.* In cat. of exhibition organised by the Société des Peintres graveurs français, November 1952, Paris, 1952

WATSON, F. J. B. *Notes on Canaletto and his engravers* (Brustolini, Visentini). In Burlington Magazine, 1950
WILDENSTEIN, G. *Fragonard aquafortiste.* Paris, Ed. Les Beaux-Arts, 1956
WILDENSTEIN, G. *Jacob Christoffel Le Blon ou le Secret de peindre en gravant.* In Gazette des Beaux-Arts, July-August 1960, Paris
WILDENSTEIN, G. *Louis Moreau.* Ed. Les Beaux-Arts, 1923
WILDENSTEIN, G. *Sur les eaux-fortes de Moreau l'aîné.* In Gazette des Beaux-Arts, December 1958
WILDENSTEIN, G. *Les caricatures révolutionnaires par David.* In Mélanges Opesco, 1962
WILDENSTEIN, G. *L'abbé de Saint-Non, artiste et mécène.* In Gazette des Beaux-Arts, May 1959
WRIGHT, TH. *The works of Gillray.* London, 1873
WRIGHT, TH. AND EVANS, R. H. *Historical account of the caricatures of Gillray.* London, 1851

ZERNER, H. *Un graveur oublié, le créateur de la manière de crayon: J.-C. François.* In Information d'Histoire de l'Art, Paris, September-October 1960
ZIGROSSER, C. *The book of fine prints.* New York, 1948

List of illustrations

Numbers in bold refer to colour plates

ANONYMOUS: *La Confrérie des Compagnons Charons*, c. 1760. Printed by Charbonnier, rue Saint-Jacques **134**
Cantique Spirituel, c. 1780. Engraved in the Letourmy workshop, Orleans **151**
Girl with a Muff. Mezzotint after Romney 153
The Triumphant Return of the Heroines: October, 1789. French engraving **173**
La Trouée de Grandpré, après Valmy, September 1792. French engraving 179
Exercise of the Rights of Man, 1792. Counter-revolutionary engraving on the subject of the September massacres 180
New Playing Cards, 1793. French engraving 182
Two Methods of Approach, 23 August 1793. French engraving . 183
Frederick William III in Full Mourning, 1793. Engraved in Delion's studio 186
Louis Capet and his family in the Temple, c. September 1792. Prudhomme, *Révolutions* 188
Robespierre guillotines the Executioner, Autumn 1794. French engraving 189
Frenchwoman going to War, 1793. German engraving 190
State of the English Nation. French engraving on the American War of Independence 217
Ha! quel vent! C'est incroyable, c. 1796. Engraving published by Bonvalet in Paris 218
Public Audience of the Directory. c. 1796. Engraved after Chataignier 219

BARTOLOZZI, FRANCESCO (1725-1815): *Venus recommending Hymen to Cupid* 222
BEAUVARLET, JACQUES-FIRMIN (1731-1797): *The Chestnut-seller*. Engraved after Greuze 128
BERTHAULT, P.-G. (1748-1819): *Revolutionary Committee under the Terror*, c. 1795. Engraved after Fragonard *jeune* 184
BEWICK, THOMAS (1753-1828): *Leopard*, from *Quadrupeds*, 1790 . 226
Sea Eagle, from *British Birds*, 1797 227

BLAKE, WILLIAM (1757-1827): *Songs of Innocence,* 1789 228
Songs of Innocence, 1789 229
BOISSIEU, JEAN-JACQUES DE (1736-1810): *The Schoolmaster* . . . 116
BONNET, LOUIS-MARIN (1736-1793): *Head of a Woman.* Engraved after Boucher. From the collection of Monsieur Baudouin, Peintre du Roi. 44
BOUCHER, FRANÇOIS (1703-1770): *Pensent-ils au raisin?* Engraved by J. P. Le Bas. 32
Les Précieuses ridicules. Illustration for Molière's play engraved by L. Cars. 33
The Charms of Country Life. Engraved by J. Daullé 34
Girl resting, 1736. Original engraving 35

CANALETTO, ANTONIO (1697-1768): *The Market in the Piazzetta, Venice* 72
Torre di Malghera 73
Venice: La Fiera del Bando 74
Portico with a Lantern 75
The Prison, Venice 76
CHODOWIECKI, DANIEL-NICOLAS (1726-1801): *Galitzine at the Battle of Choczin* 145
The Emotional Responses of the Four Temperaments, c. 1767 . . . 146
Calas' Last Farewell, c. 1767 147
CHOFFARD, PIERRE-PHILIPPE (1730-1809): *Allegory.* Engraved by Gautier-Dagoty 50
Vignette for a Ball 51
CHRÉTIEN, GILLES-LOUIS (1754-1811): *Portrait of Le Pelletier de Saint-Fargeau,* 1792 221
COCHIN PÈRE, CHARLES-NICOLAS (1688-1754): *Le Jeu du Pied de Bœuf.* Engraved after de Troy 22
COCHIN FILS, CHARLES-NICOLAS (1715-90): *The Ladies' Tailor,* 1737. 36
Madame du Deffand's Persian Cats, 1746 37
Funeral of the Dauphine, Maria Teresa of Spain, 1748. 38
An Experiment with Electricity, c. 1739. 39
The Patcher, c. 1737. Engraved by Ravenet 40
Mésangère Sale Catalogue. 41
The Genie of Medals, c. 1737 42
CRUICKSHANK, ISAAC (1756-1816): *John am I Draggl'd* 195

DAULLÉ, JEAN (1703-1763): *Louis XV, King of France.* Engraved after Rigaud 52
DAVID, LOUIS (1748-1825): *The Great Royal Knife-Grinding Establishment for sharpening English Swords,* May 1794 199
DEBUCOURT, PHILIBERT-LOUIS (1755-1832): *The Ill-guarded Rose,* 1791 162
The Two Kisses, 1786 171
DELAFOSSE, JEAN-BAPTISTE (born 1721): *The Unfortunate Calas Family,* 1765. Engraved after Carmontelle 149
DE LAUNAY, NICOLAS (1739-1792): *The Indiscreet Wife.* Engraved after Baudouin 159
DEMARTEAU, GILLES (1722-1776): *Nude.* Engraved after Boucher. Dedicated to Monsieur Bergeret, Collector of Taxes 123
Head of a Woman. Engraved after Boucher 132
Nude. Engraved after Boucher 137
DENON, VIVANT (1747-1825): *Breakfast at Ferney.* Engraved by Née and Masquelier 117
Self-portrait 119
DREVET, PIERRE-IMBERT (1697-1739): *Bossuet.* Engraved after Rigaud 56
DUCREUX, JOSEPH (1735-1802): *Ducreux distressed,* February 1791. Engraved by himself in England 210

EISEN, CHARLES-DOMINIQUE (1720-1778): *Vignette.* Engraved by J. de Longueil 48
Vignette. Engraved by J. de Longueil 49

FRAGONARD, HONORE (1732-1806): *The Swing,* 1782. Engraved by De Launay 94
The Closet, 1778. Original engraving. 95
La Chemise Enlevée, 1787. Engraved by Geursant 96
Satyrs playing, 1763. Original engraving 97
Bacchanalia, 1763. Original engraving 97
The Stubborn Donkey. Engraved by Saint-Non 98
La Culbute, 1766. Engraved by F. P. Charpentier 99
La Chiffre d'Amour, 1787. Engraved by De Launay. 100
The Little Park, c. 1763. Original engraving. 103

GAMELIN (1738-1803): Plate from the *Nouveau Recueil d'Ostéologie et de Myologie* 176

GÉRARD, MARGUERITE (1761-1837): *The Child and the Bulldog,* c. 1780. Engraved with Fragonard. 112
GILLRAY, JAMES (1757-1815): *French Liberty. British Slavery* . . . 193
The Gradual Abolition of the Slave Trade, c. 1793. Caricature of the French 195
The Finishing Touch, September 1791. 196
The Zenith of French Glory 197
Un petit Souper à la Parisienne, or, *A Family of Sansculottes refreshing after the Fatigues of the Day,* 1793. 199
GOYA, FRANCISCO DE (1746-1828): *It is hot. Caprichos,* No. 13. . 200
They say Yes... Caprichos, No. 2. 202
Good Advice. Caprichos, No. 15 203
It is pulled well up. Caprichos, No. 17. 204
Even looking thus, he cannot yet see. Caprichos, No. 7 205
This Dust! Caprichos, No. 23 206
San Francisco de Paula, c. 1770 207
Poor little things! Caprichos, No. 22 208
How they pluck her. Caprichos, No. 21 209
GRAVELOT, HUBERT-FRANÇOIS (1699-1773): *Electricity* 46
The Absent-minded Man. Illustration for an edition of La Bruyère 47
GUÉRARD, NICOLAS: *The villager,* c. 1710. 27
GUYARD (working c. 1780): *But at the First Sound of the Drum...,* c. 1794. Engraved after Mallet 181

HOGARTH, WILLIAM (1694-1764): *The Company of Undertakers,* 1736. 58
The Rake's Progress, V: *He Marries an Old Maid* 60
A Harlot's Progress, I: *Her arrival in London* 63
Beer Street, 1751 64
First Stage of Cruelty 67
HUBER, JEAN (1721-1786): *The Philosophers at Supper* 125
Portrait of Voltaire 126
Mademoiselle Clairon's Visit to Ferney. 127

JACKSON, JOHN BAPTIST (1700-c. 1780): *The Meal.* After a Venetian engraving 138

JANINET, JEAN-FRANÇOIS (1752-1814): *Colonnade and Gardens of the Medici Palace.* Engraved after Hubert Robert 175

LALIVE DE JULLY, ANGE LAURENT DE (1725-1779): *Self-portrait,* c. 1760 115
LANCRET, NICOLAS (1690-1743): *Quoi n'avez-vous point?...* Engraved by M. M. Horthemels, wife of Cochin *père* 20
Dans cette Aimable Solitude... Engraved by Cochin *père* 21
LAVREINCE, NICOLAS (1737-1807): *The Love-Letter.* Engraved by De Launay 156
The Happy Moment. Engraved by De Launay 157
LE BLON, JACOB-CHRISTOPH (1667-1741): *Portrait of Louis XV.* Engraved after Blackey 140
LEDOUX, CLAUDE-NICOLAS (1736-1806): Plate from *Architecture* 225
LEGRAND, A. (1765-1815): *Reception of the Decree of the 18th Floréal.* Engraved after Debucourt. 1794, second state of a print entitled *Vive le Roy,* published in July 1794. A third state, in 1797, proclaimed *The Joy of the French Nation at the Announcement of the Peace Treaty with Europe* 187
LÉPICIÉ, BERNARD (1699-1755): *The Busy Mother,* 1744. Engraved after Chardin 131
LEPRINCE, JEAN-BAPTISTE (1734-1781): *Russian Concert,* c. 1770 142
LOUVION, JEAN-BAPTISTE (1740-1804): *The Ninth Thermidor or the English Surprise,* 27 July 1794 185

MOREAU L'AINÉ, LOUIS (1740-1806): *The Foot-bridge* 109
The Cottage 109
MOREAU LE JEUNE, JEAN-MICHEL (1741-1814): *The Magic Lantern Show.* Engraved by Martini 155
Last words of Jean-Jacques Rousseau. Engraved by Gutenberg . . 165
The Farewell. Engraved by De Launay 166
The Gardens of Marly. Engraved by Gutenberg 167
The Queen's Lady in Waiting. Engraved by P. A. Martini . . . 168
Illuminations for the Marriage of Louis XVI 169
It's a Boy, Monsieur! Engraved by C. Baquoy 170

NATTIER, JEAN-MARC (1685-1766): *Night departs and Dawn appears.* Engraved by Pierre Maleuvre 24
NORBLIN DE LA GOURDAINE, JEAN-PIERRE (1745-1830): *Susannah and the Elders,* 1776 114

OUDRY, JEAN-BAPTISTE (1686-1755): *Deer at Bay* 30
The Frogs who wanted a King. Engraved by Chedel 31

PAPILLON, JEAN-MICHEL (1698-1776): *Vignette engraved on Wood* 55
PIRANESI, GIAMBATTISTA (1720-1778): *Prison Scene from the Carceri* 87
Prison Scene from the Carceri 88
Prison Scene from the Carceri 89
Rome: the Pantheon 90
Rome: the Forum of Nerva 90
POMPADOUR, MADAME DE (1721-1764): *Child,* 1751 113
PRUD'HON, PIERRE-PAUL (1758-1823): *The Bath.* Engraved by Roger 223
Phrosyne and Melidore 224

ROBERT, HUBERT (1733-1808): *Evening in Rome: The Sarcophagus* 118
ROWLANDSON, THOMAS (1756-1827): *Transplanting of Teeth* . . **192**
Fast Day 198

SAINT-AUBIN, AUGUSTIN DE (1736-1807): *Madame de Pompadour,* 1764. Engraved after Cochin. 102
At least be discreet! 110
You may count on me! 111
SAINT-AUBIN, GABRIEL DE (1724-1780): *L'Académie Particulière* 101
Le Salon du Louvre, 1753. 104
The Procession of the Fatted Ox 105
The Two Lovers 106
A Conference of Lawyers 107
Les Nouvellistes, 1752 108
SAINT-AUBIN, GERMAIN DE (1721-1786): *Butterfly Fantasies: Pyrotechny* 92
Butterfly Fantasies: The Tight-rope Walker 93
SAINT-MESMIN, JULIEN FEVRET DE (1770-1852): *Portrait of Levington* 220
SCHMIDT, GEORGES-FRÉDÉRIC (1712-1775): *Louis de La Tour d'Auvergne, Comte d'Evreux,* 1739 130
SERGENT MARCEAU, ANTOINE (1751-1847): *The Happy Mother* . 178

TIEBOUT, CORNELIUS (c. 1777-c.1830): *West Point* 215
TIEPOLO, GIOVANNI BATTISTA (1692-1770): *Adoration of the Magi*. 78
The Tomb of Punchinello 81
Capriccio 82

Man with a Horse 83
Flight into Egypt 85

VOYSARD, ETIENNE CLAUDE (1746-1812): *The Cavalry Sergeant Gillet.* Engraved after Borel 160

WATTEAU, ANTOINE (1684-1721): *Italian Costumes.* Original engraving. First state 12
Departure of the Italian Actors. Engraved by L. Jacob 13
Costume Study. Original engraving 14
Seated Woman. Original engraving. 15
A Ride on a Sledge. Engraved by Boucher 16
Recruits going to join the Regiment. Original engraving. 17
The Anxious Sweetheart. Engraved by P. Aveline 18
WRIGHT, JOSEPH (1756-1793): *Portrait of Washington* 216

Index of Names

Ackermann, Rudolph, 139
Adam, Robert, 91
Adhémar, Mme, 13
Alba, Duchess of, 211
Allabre, Guillaume, 141
Amigoni, Jacopo, 121
Amstel, Ploos van, 135
Angoulême, Duke of, 158
Antal, 70, 145
Ariosto, 148
Arnavon, 141
Artois, Count of, 158
Artois, Countess of, 158
Atkinson, Thomas, 233
Audran, Gérard, 26
Audran, Jean, 19, 23, 28, 45
Austin, W., 139

Bachaumont, 45
Balechou, 9
Baron, Bernard, 68
Barrocel, 98
Barry, Mme du, 163
Bartolozzi, Francesco, 218, 222
Bartsch, 234
Basan, P.-F., 124, 172, 234
Basire, James, 68
Basset, 143
Baudelaire, Charles, 91
Baudouin, 8, 154, 159, 163, 234
Beaumarchais, 148
Beauvarlet, Jacques-Firmin, 28, 121, 128
Bella, Stefano della, 84, 114
Bellegarde, Mme de, 158
Bellotto, Bernardo, 77
Bermudez, Cean, 79
Bernard, Samuel, 23
Berthault, 184
Berti, 234
Bervic, 172
Bewick, Thomas, 22, 226, 227
Bibiena, 86
Binyon, Lawrence, 236
Blake, William, 225, 228, 229
Blackey, 136
Bléry, 116
Blum, André, 183
Blumenbach, 147
Boccaccio, 53
Boileau, 32
Boilly, 171
Boissieu, Jean-Jacques de, 112, 114, 116
Boizot, 158
Bonaparte, Lucien, 230
Bonaparte, Napoleon, 158, 161, 194
Bonnart, 14
Bonnet, Louis-Marin, 45, 135
Bonneval, de, 45
Bonvalet, 218
Bord, 133
Borel, 160
Bosse, Abraham, 233
Bouchard, 88
Boucher, François, 8, 19, 29, 32-35, 40, 45, 99, 106, 122, 125, 129, 132, 135, 137, 139, 154, 161, 234
Bouchot, 236
Bounieu, 177
Bourcard, 236
Bowles, 69
Boydell, 68, 150, 172
Boyer de Nîmes, 188
Bracquemond, 116
Brooks, 136
Brookshaw, Richard, 121
Bruand, Yves, 98
Bruandet, 114
Brühl, Count, 143
Brunet, 57
Buffon, 147
Bünau, Count, 143
Burdett P. P., 139
Burty, Philippe, 235
Byrne, 172

Calas, Jean, 144, 145, 149, 150

Callot, 11, 15, 59, 114
Canaletto, Antonio, 71-79
Canot, 121
Carlevarijs, 74, 75
Carmona, Salvador, 201
Carmontelle, 145, 149
Cars, François, 25
Cars, Gabriel, 25
Cars, Jean, 25
Cars, Jean-François, 25, 26
Cars, Laurent 25, 26, 28, 33, 42, 122
Cassas, 176
Castel-Courval, 55, 57
Castiglione, 84
Caylus, Count of, 133
Charbonnier, 135
Chardin, Jean Baptiste Siméon, 28, 121, 122, 131
Charles III of Spain, 201, 209
Charles IV of Spain, 209
Charpentier, François-Philippe, 99, 139
Chataignier, 219
Chedel, 31
Chéreau, 23, 143
Chevigné, Davy de, 158
Chodowiecki, Daniel-Nicolas, 8, 69, 122, 143-150, 152, 174
Chodowiecki, Wilhelm, 144
Choffard, Pierre-Philippe, 50, 51, 54, 57, 59, 201
Choiseul-Gouffier, 176
Chrétien, Gilles-Louis, 215, 217, 221
Christophe, 26
Cipriani, 218
Clérisseau, 91
Clubbe, John, 69
Cochin, Abbé de, 108
Cochin, Charles-Nicolas, *père*, 22, 25, 26, 29, 43
Cochin, Charles-Nicolas, *fils,* 10, 36-43, 45-47, 51-53, 55, 104, 122, 143, 150, 161, 163, 174, 233
Colette, 236
Conrad, Zacharias, 143
Corneille, Pierre, 106
Costa, Gianfrancesco, 77
Courboin, 236
Coypel, 37, 98, 122
Cranach, 127
Crébillon, 229
Crépy, 141
Crozat, Antoine, 124
Crozat, Pierre, 17, 19, 124, 125
Cruikshank, Isaac, 194, 195
Curtis, Atherton, 88

d'Abbeville, Delattré, 233
Dacier, 101, 139
d'Agincourt, 54
Dagoty, Gautier, 139, 233
d'Alembert, 230
d'Argenville, Dezallier, 129
Daudet, 119
Daullé, Jean, 34, 52
Daumont, 143
David, Charles, 25
David, Edwin, 215
David, Jacques Louis, 117, 185, 189, 228
d'Azaincourt, Blondel, 132, 135
Debucourt, Philibert-Louis, 8, 152, 154, 162, 164, 171, 172, 174, 177, 187, 191, 212, 213
Delacroix, Eugène, 214
Delafosse, Jean-Baptiste, 145, 148
De Launay, Nicolas, 8, 94, 100, 119, 154, 156, 157, 159, 165, 166
Delion, 186
Demarteau, Gilles, 40, 122, 129, 130, 132, 133, 135, 137, 213
Denmark, King of, 172
Denon, Vivant, 112, 115, 117, 119, 214
Dent, 194
Despiez, 179
Diderot, Denis, 48, 51, 70, 135, 230, 231
Didot, Firmin, 229, 234
Didot, Pierre, *the elder,* 226, 229
Doissin, Louis, 233
Donie, Robert, 233
Dorat, 54, 55, 57, 163

Dostoievsky, Fëdor Mikhailovich, 211
Drevet, Pierre, *père*, 26, 28
Drevet, Pierre-Imbert, 28, 56, 143
Duchange, Gaspard, 19
Duchesne, 177
Duclos, 119, 158, 165
Ducreux, 210, 212
Duplessis, 165, 171
Dupuis, Nicolas-Gabriel, 116, 201
Dürer, Albrecht, 11
Dyck, van, 108

Eberts, Jean-Henri, 163
Edelinck, 25, 121
Egalité, Philippe, Duke of Chartres, 232
Eisen, Charles-Dominique, 48, 49, 53-55, 57, 161
Engelbrecht d'Augsbourg, Martin, 23
Erman, 147
Escoquiz, Juan de, 208

Faldoni, 121
Faure, Elie, 61
Ficquet, Etienne, 9, 172
Fielding, 69
Firens, Gaspard, 25
Firens, Marthe, 25
Firens, Pierre, 25
Fleming, 122
Flipart, 122
Floding, 139
Focillon, Henri, 236
Foinvelle, Nicolas, 144
Fontanelle, 48
Fouquet, 217
Fournier, 217
Fragonard, Honoré, 84, 85, 91, 94-100, 103, 112, 120, 125, 129, 139, 171, 184, 213, 234
François, Jean-Charles, 133, 135, 213, 218, 226
Frederick II, 143, 144
Frederick William III, 186
Freundenberger (Freundeberg), Sigmund, 163, 164
Frietzsche, 72
Fuseli, Henry, 233

Gaillard, 122
Gamelin, 8, 176
Gaucher, 116, 124, 163
Gauguin, Paul, 141
Gellert, 148
Gentil-Bernard, 226
Gérard, 226, 229
Gérard, Marguerite, 229
Gérard, Mme, 98
Gersaint, 233
Gessner, 148
Ghuy, Marcenay de, 112
Gillet, Louis, Cavalry Sergeant, 160
Gillot, Claude, 15, 32, 37
Gillray, James, 9, 70, 177, 191, 193-198, 212, 230
Gilpin, William, 234
Girodet de Roucy-Trioson, 226, 229
Goday, 201, 211, 214, 232
Gogh, Vincent van, 76
Goldsmith, Oliver, 148
Goncourt (brothers), 48, 53, 54, 120, 165, 177, 188, 234, 235
Goya, Francisco de, 8, 80, 84, 194, 200-209, 211, 212, 214, 234
Gravelot, Hubert-François, 46, 47, 51, 53, 54, 161
Gray, Basil, 191
Green, Valentine, 136, 150
Greuze, Jean Baptiste, 28, 121, 122, 124, 128, 145
Grignion, Charles, 68
Grimm, 26, 55
Guardi, Francesco, 77, 79
Guay, 106
Guérard, 27
Guersant, 96
Gutenberg, 165
Guyard, 181, 188
Guyot, 158

Heinecken, 234

Henri IV, 141, 158
Heusy, de, 130
Heyne, Gottlieb, 143
Hind, 80, 83, 84, 86, 236
Hogarth, William, 8, 57, 60-70, 145, 146, 191, 233
Hollande, 191
Honnet, 230
Hoyau, 141
Huber, Jean, 8, 125-127, 174
Huet, Paul, 135
Humbert, Abraham von, 233
Huquier, 124

Iriarte, 207
Isabey, Jean Baptiste, 8

Jabach, 124
Jackson, John Baptiste, 136, 233
Janinet, Jean-François, 154, 175
Jaucourt, Chevalier de, 230
Jeaurat, 135
Jombert, 47, 233
Joubert, 141
Joullain *fils*, 91
Jovellanos, 208, 216
Jullienne, Jean de, 17, 19, 23, 129

Kauffmann, Angelica, 218
Kirkall, Elisha, 69, 136
Knapton, 133

Laan, 218
La Borde, Benjamin de, 163, 176
La Bretonne, Restif de, 164
Lacombe, 19
La Fage, 11
La Fayette, 191
La Fontaine, 31, 37, 43, 57, 226
La Force, Piganiol de, 129
Lafrensen, Nicolas, 154
La Gordaine, Norblin de, 112, 114
Lajoue, 54
Laline de Jully, A. L., 108, 115
Lalive, 23
La Motte, 37
Lancret, Nicolas, 15, 20, 21, 28, 122
Landry, 141
Larmessin, 141
Lavater, Johann Kasper, 145, 150, 172, 174, 212, 213
Laveaux, 147
Laver, James, 194
Lavreince, 8, 152, 154, 156, 157, 235
Le Bas, J. P., 26, 32, 53, 120, 121, 163, 171, 174
Leblanc, Abbé, 43
Le Blon, Jacob Christophe, 136, 139, 140, 233
Leblond, 141
Le Brun, 23, 26, 122
Leclerc, Sébastien, 233
Legrand, A., 187
Lemoyne, François, 23, 25, 26, 28, 42, 125
Lempereur, 28, 124
Lépicié, Bernard, 122, 131
Leprince, Jean-Baptiste, 139, 142
Lesage, 148
Le Sueur, Hubert, 122
Lessing, 148
Letourny, 141
Levasseur, 122
Lhorente, 203, 208
Lievens, 114
Longueil, J. de, 48, 49, 54
Loo, Carle van, 28
Lorrain, Claude le, 11, 98
Lorrain, Robert le, 161
Louis XIV, 11, 23, 232
Louis XV, 37, 43, 52, 57, 86, 106, 136, 139, 140, 154, 163, 177, 232
Louis XVI, 57, 121, 152, 154, 158, 161, 163, 169, 171, 172, 177, 184, 232
Louvion, 185

MacArdell, 136
Maffei, 84
Magny, 133
Maintenon, Mme de, 9

Major, Thomas, 68
Maleuvre, Pierre, 24
Mallet, 181, 188
Malraux, André, 201, 213
Marat, Jean Paul, 184
Marceau, Sergent, 178
Marie-Antoinette, 158, 179, 184, 185
Marie-Louise, Archduchess of Austria, 158
Marieschi, 74, 75
Mariette, Pierre J., 11, 13, 15, 108, 122, 124, 141, 231
Marigny, 43, 70
Marillier, 57, 226
Marmontel, 53
Marot, 86
Martinez, 201
Martini, 155, 174
Martyn, Thomas, 233
Masquelier, Louis-Joseph, 19, 117, 176
Massard, 122
Massard, Louise, 158
Meissonier, 54
Melini, 121
Mellan, 121
Mercier, Philippe, 7, 15, 141, 152
Meryon, 116
Messerschmidt, 212
Meyer, 72
Miger, 124
Mirabeau, Honoré Gabriel Riqueti, Count, 211
Mire, Le, 54
Moitte, 229
Molière, 33, 40, 226
Mondhare, 141, 143
Monnet, 226
Montenault de, 37, 39
Montesquieu, Charles Louis de Secondat, 226
Moratin, 42, 201
Moreau, Jean-Michel, *le Jeune,* 10, 150, 152, 154, 155, 158, 161, 163-170, 226, 234
Moreau, Louis, *l'Aîné*, 104, 109, 161
Morellon La Cave, François, 68
Morghen, Raphael, 169, 201
Mosley, Charles, 68
Müller, Johan Gothard, 171, 172

Nanteuil, 25, 26
Nattier, Jean-Marc, 24
Natoire, 98
Naudet, 105
Née, François-Denis, 117, 176
Nichols, John, 233
Nicolaï, 147
Nolin, 141
Nuñuz, Fernan, 211

Octavien, 13, 15
Olavides, Governor of Andalusia and Seville, 211
Orleans, Duke of, 155
Oudry, Jean-Baptiste, 29-31, 37, 43

Paez de Santiago, Elena, 201
Paignon-Dijonval, 231
Pannini, 45
Palluchini, 71, 72, 74, 76
Papillon, Jean-Michel, 40, 55, 57, 59, 233
Pasquier, 141
Pater, Jean Baptiste Joseph, 15
Paufi, 25
Perrault, 108
Peter the Great, 148
Peyron, 229
Picart, Bernard, 23, 29, 32, 121
Pierre, 141
Pine, John, 121
Pinel, 203
Piranesi, Gianbattista, 71, 80, 86-91, 213, 234
Pittaluga, Mme, 75
Pognon, Edmond, 28
Pompadour, Mme de, 43, 106, 108, 113
Ponce, 158
Pond, Arthur, 133
Porporati, 172
Poussin, 122

Prault, 163
Preissler, 171, 172
Priola, Marquis de, 235
Prouté, Paul, 66, 104
Prudhomme, 188
Prud'hon, Pierre-Paul, 8, 219, 223, 224, 226, 228, 230

Quenedey, 215, 217
Queverdo, 226
Quillard, 15

Racine, Jean, 228
Rakewell, Thomas, 61
Raphael, 127
Ravenet, Simon-François, 40, 68, 121
Réau, Louis, 49
Reclam, 147
Regnault, 219, 226
Rembrandt, Harmensz van Rijn, 7, 11, 70, 82, 86, 91, 93, 95, 108, 112, 114, 233
Revere, Paul, 215
Reynolds, Sir Joshua, 8, 136, 143, 150
Reynolds, Samuel William, 150
Ribera, Salvator Rosa, 84
Ricci, Marco, 74, 75
Richardson, 147, 230
Rigaud, Hyacinthe, 9, 19, 28, 52, 57
Robert, Hubert, 118, 175
Robespierre, 181
Robin, 183
Rochefort, 141
Roger, 223
Romney, 153
Rouquet, 70
Rousseau, Jean-Jacques, 108, 148, 163, 165, 211
Rowlandson, Thomas, 70, 174, 177, 188, 191, 192, 194, 198, 212-214
Rubens, Sir Peter Paul, 19, 54
Ryland, William Wynne, 9, 121, 172, 218

Sack, 79, 80
Sade, Marquis de, 158
Saint-Agathe, 141
Saint-Aubin, Augustin de, 102, 103, 108, 110, 111, 120, 194
Saint-Aubin, Gabriel de, 99, 101, 103-108, 194
Saint-Aubin, Germain de, 91-93, 103, 194
Saint-Florentin, Count of, 169
Saint-Mesmin, Fevret de, 217, 220
Saint-Non, Abbé de, 98, 112, 176
Salmon, 155
Sartine, de, 132
Sayers, 194
Saxe-Teschen, Duke of, 169
Saxe-Teschen, Prince of, 125, 169
Schiller, 148
Schmidt, Georg Friedrich, 130, 135, 172
Schmuzer, 172
Scotin, Louis-Gérard, 68
Seguin, M. and Mme, 141
Sevestre, 141
Shakespeare, William, 148
Sieyès, Abbé, 152
Silvestre, Israël, 59
Simonneau, Ch., 15, 19
Simonet, 119, 158
Smith, Joseph, 71
Smith, J. R., 136, 150, 172
Soldtz brothers, 45, 46
Soubeyran, 121
Soufflot, 43
Spilsbury, Francis, 13, 233
Spooner, 69
Sterne, 148
Strange, Sir Robert, 121
Stubbs, George, 219, 222
Sullivan, Luke, 68

Taine, 234
Taraval, 158
Tardieu, 19, 139, 172
Taylor, Basil, 222
Teniers, David I., 54, 121, 122
Tersan, Abbé Campion de, 152
Tessin, 124, 125

Tiepolo, Gian Domenico, 79, 84
Tiepolo, Giovanni Battista, 71-86, 89, 98, 213
Tiepolo, Lorenzo, 79, 84
Tiebout, Cornelius, 215
Tocqué, 169
Torcheboeuf, 141
Trouvain, 141
Troy, de, 16, 22, 23
Tolnay, Charles de, 127

Uffenbach, Johann Friedrich von, 143
Urquijo, 211

Valdès, Melendez, 207, 209
Valory, Chevalier de, 23
Vangelisti, 121, 161
Vanneck, 141
Vauvermans, 122
Velasquez, Diego Rodriguez de Silva, 201
Vernet (family), 174
Vèze, M. de, 234
Vien, Joseph, 91
Vincent, 232
Vinci, Leonardo da, 212
Visprė, F. X., 150
Vliet, van, 114
Volpato, 201
Voltaire, François-Marie Arouet, 120, 144, 148, 158, 174, 211, 230
Voysard, 160

Walpole, Horace, 65, 136, 233
Watelet, Claude-Henri, 26, 108
Watteau, Antoine, 11-19, 23, 26, 37, 42, 53, 116, 125, 129, 133, 134
Watteau, Pierre-Jean, 13
Weigert, M. R. A., 25
Weirotter, 172
Weisbrodt, Charles, 119
Wicar, 19, 177
Wildenstein, M. G., 85, 136, 139
Wille, *fils*, 8, 158, 121, 163, 164
Winckelmann, 143
Woolet, William, 68
Wright, Joseph, 215, 216

Young, 208

Zanetti, Anton Maria, 79, 121